Guardian Angels

GUARDIAN
ANGELS

Fifteen new stories by winners of the
Guardian Children's Fiction Award.

Edited by Stephanie Nettell

Illustrated by Mike Daley

VIKING KESTREL

Penguin Books Ltd, Harmondsworth, Middlesex, England
Viking Penguin Inc., 40 West 23rd Street, New York, New York 10010, U.S.A.
Penguin Books Australia Ltd, Ringwood, Victoria, Australia
Penguin Books Canada Limited, 2801 John Street, Markham, Ontario, Canada L3R 1B4
Penguin Books (N.Z.) Ltd, 182–190 Wairau Road, Auckland 10, New Zealand

First published 1987

Typeset in 12/14 pt. Ehrhardt

Printed in Great Britain by Richard Clay Ltd, Bungay, Suffolk

British Library Cataloguing in Publication Data

Guardian angels: fifteen new stories by
winners of the Guardian Children's Fiction
Award
1. Children's stories, English
I. Nettell, Stephanie II. The Guardian
823'.01'089282 [J]   PZ5

ISBN 0-670-81077-0

Contents

Winners of the *Guardian* Children's Fiction Award

Introduction

Here is a celebration. This year, 1987, the *Guardian* Children's Fiction Award is twenty years old – and this anthology is rather like a birthday party where all sorts of guests who have won the award in the past are sitting around after a splendid meal, making up stories. As you would expect, they're all brilliant storytellers and it's a really good party!

You may already know the *Guardian* is a very old and famous British newspaper, but I wonder what the actual word 'guardian' makes you think of? Because that was the question I asked these writers (let's say when we were cutting the cake), and being the clever, original and idiosyncratic bunch that they are, they answered in an extraordinary and exciting variety of ways. Their stories are as surprising and as different from each other as the writers themselves.

7

They are daftly funny or touchingly sad; they take place thousands of years ago, sixty years ago and today; they offer teasing fantasy and bitter reality, soaring myth and literal truth.

And they are – amazingly so, I think – very characteristic of their authors, so if you find yourself enjoying one by a writer whose name you haven't come across before, there is every chance that you would also get pleasure from his or her novels. Some of these authors have written both easy and tough books, or for both young children and teenagers, but any librarian or knowledgeable bookseller will point you in the right direction. Discovering a good writer in this way is one of the special joys of reading.

It is also, of course, the aim of any award not only to praise an outstanding book but, if possible, to introduce a new or lesser known author to a wider public. Although award-winners may already be established writers, in the world of children's books there is always a new generation of readers with the pleasure of discovery still to come.

The four judges of the *Guardian* Children's Fiction Award must themselves be children's writers (sometimes the winners have gone on to serve as judges). They know about good writing, and they know children. A glance at the award's roll of honour vouches for their judgement: after twenty years all the winners are still names to conjure with, and they are all still writing.

They're writing good stuff, too. Stories like the ones in this collection. As I said, it's a brilliant party – do join us. I promise you'll have fun.

Stephanie Nettell
Children's Books Editor
The *Guardian*

A Grave Misunderstanding

LEON GARFIELD

I am a dog. I think you ought to know right away. I don't want to save it up for later, because you might begin to wonder what sort of a person it was who went about on all fours, sniffing at bottoms and peeing up against lampposts in the public street. You wouldn't like it; and I don't suppose you'd care to have anything more to do with me.

The truth of the matter is, we have different standards, me and my colleagues, that is; not in everything, I hasten to bark, but in enough for it to be noticeable. For instance, although we are as fond of a good walk as the next person, love puppies and smoked salmon, we don't go much on reading. We find it hard to turn the pages. But, on the other paw, a good deep snoutful of mingled air as it comes humming off a rubbish dump can be as teasing to us as a sonnet. Indeed,

9

there are rhymes in rancid odours such as you'd never dream
of; and every puddle tells a story.

We see things, too. Only the other day, when me and my
Person were out walking, and going as brisk as biscuits,
through that green and quiet place of marble trees and stony,
lightless lampposts, where people bury their bones and never
dig them up, I saw a ghost. I stopped. I glared, I growled,
my hair stood up on end –

'What the devil's the matter with you now?' demanded
my Person.

'What a beautiful dog!' said the ghost, who knew that I
knew what she was, and that we both knew that my Person
did not.

She was the lifeless, meaningless shell of a young female
person whose bones lay not very far away. No heart beat
within her, there was wind in her veins, and she smelled of
worm-crumble and pine.

'Thank you,' said my Person, with a foolishly desiring
smile: for the ghost's eyes were very come-hitherish, even
though her hither was thither, under the grass. 'He *is* rather a
handsome animal. Best of breed at Cruft's you know.' The
way to his heart was always open through praise of me.

'Does he bite?' asked the ghost, watching me with all the
empty care of nothingness trying to be something.

'SHE'S DEAD – SHE'S DEAD!'

'Stop barking!' said my Person. 'Don't be frightened. He
wouldn't hurt a fly. Do you come here often?'

'Every day,' murmured the ghost, with a sly look towards
her bones. She moved a little nearer to my Person. A breeze
sprang up, and I could smell it blowing right through her,
like frozen flowers. 'He looks very fierce,' said the ghost. 'Are
you sure that he's kind?'

'COME AWAY – COME AWAY!'

'Stop barking!' commanded my Person, and looked at the ghost with springtime in his eyes. If only he could have smelled the dust inside her head, and heard the silence inside her breast! But it was no good. All he could see was a silken smile. He was only a person, and blindly trusted his eyes ...

'Dogs', said the ghost, 'should be kept on a lead in the churchyard. There's a notice on the gate.' She knew that I knew where she was buried, and that I'd just been going to dig up her bones.

My Person obeyed; and the ghost looked at me as if to say, 'Now you'll never be able to show him that I'm dead!'

'SHE'S COLD! SHE'S EMPTY! SHE'S GRANDDAUGHTER DEATH!'

'Stop barking!' shouted my Person, and, dragging me after, walked on, already half in love with the loveless ghost.

We passed very close to her bones. I could smell them, and I could hear the little nibblers dryly rustling. I pulled, I strained, I jerked to dig up her secret ...

'He looks so wild!' said the ghost. 'His eyes are rolling and his jaws are dripping. Are you sure he doesn't have a fever? Don't you think he ought to go to the vet?'

'He only wants to run off and play,' said my Person. 'Do you live near here?'

'YES! YES! RIGHT BY THAT MARBLE LAMPPOST! SIX PAWS DEEP IN THE EARTH!'

'Stop barking!' said my Person. 'Do you want to wake up the dead?'

The ghost started. Then she laughed, like the wind among rotting leaves. 'I have a room nearby,' she murmured. 'A little room all to myself. It is very convenient, you know.'

'A little room all to yourself?' repeated my Person, his heart beating with eager concern. 'How lonely that must be!'

'Yes,' she said. 'Sometimes it is very lonely in my little

room, even though I hear people walking and talking up-stairs, over my head.'

'Then let me walk back with you,' said my Person; 'and keep you company!'

'No dogs allowed,' said the ghost. 'They would turn me out, you know.'

'Then come my way!' said my Person; and the ghost raised her imitation eyebrows in imitation surprise. 'Madam will you walk,' sang my Person laughingly. 'Madam will you talk, Madam will you walk and talk with me?'

'I don't see why not,' smiled the ghost.

'BECAUSE SHE'S DEAD — DEAD — DEAD!'

'Stop barking!' said my Person. ' "I will give you the keys of Heaven, I will give you the keys of my heart . . ." '

'The keys of Heaven?' sighed the ghost. 'Would you really?'

'And the keys of my heart! Will you have dinner with me?'

'Are you inviting me into your home?'

'NO GHOSTS ALLOWED! SHE'LL TURN ME OUT!'

'Stop barking! Yes . . . if you'd like to!'

'Oh I would indeed — I would indeed!'

'DON'T DO IT! YOU'LL BE BRINGING DEATH INTO OUR HOME!'

'For God's sake, stop that barking! This way . . . this way . . .'

It was hopeless, hopeless! There was only one thing left for a dog to do. *She* knew what it was, of course: she could see it in my eyes. She walked on the other side of my Person, and always kept him between herself and me. I bided my time . . .

'Do you like Italian food?' asked my Person.

'Not spaghetti,' murmured the ghost. 'It reminds me of worms.'

It was then that I broke free. I jerked forward with all my strength and wrenched the lead from out of my Person's grasp. He shouted! The ghost glared and shrank away. For a moment I stared into her eyes, and she stared into mine.

'Dogs must be kept on a lead!' whispered the ghost as I jumped. 'There's a notice on ... on ... on ...'

It was like jumping through cobwebs and feathers; and when I turned, she'd vanished like a puff of air. I saw the grass shiver, and I knew she'd gone back to her bones.

'SHE WAS DEAD! SHE WAS DEAD! I TOLD YOU SO!'

My Person didn't answer. He was shaking, he was trembling; for the very first time, he couldn't believe his eyes.

'What happened? Where — where is she? Where has she gone?'

I showed him. Trailing my lead, I went to where she lay, six paws under, and began to dig.

'No! No!' he shrieked. 'For God's sake, let her lie there in peace!'

Thankfully I stopped. The earth under the grass was thick and heavy, and the going was hard. I went back to my Person. He had collapsed on a bench and was holding his head in his hands. I tried to comfort him by licking his ear.

A female person walked neatly by. She was young and smooth and shining, and smelled of coffee and cats. She was dressed in the softest of white.

'Oh, what a beautiful dog,' she said, pausing to admire me.

He stared up at her. His eyes widened; his teeth began to chatter. He could not speak.

'GO ON! GO ON! "BEST OF BREED AT CRUFTS'S!"'

'Hush!' said the female person, reproaching me with a gentle smile. 'You'll wake up the dead!'

'Is she real?' whispered my Person, his eyes as wide and

round as tins. 'Or is she a ghost? Show me, show me! Try to jump through her like you did before! Jump, jump!'

'BUT SHE'S REAL! SHE'S ALIVE!'

'Stop barking and jump!'

So I jumped. She screamed – but not in fright. She screamed with rage. My paws were still thick and filthy with churchyard mud, and, in a moment, so was her dress.

'You – you madman!' she shouted at my shamefaced Person. 'You told him to do it! You told him to jump! You're not fit to have a dog!'

'But – but –' he cried out as she stormed away, to report him, she promised, to the churchyard authorities and the RSPCA.

'I TOLD YOU SHE WAS ALIVE! I TOLD YOU SO!'

'Stop barking!' wept my Person. 'Please!'

A Rhyme for Silver

JOAN AIKEN

EIGHTEEN-YEAR-OLD Jeff Tichborne worked in Goodman's TV and Radio Repair department. His younger brother Simon always enjoyed passing the shop-window, which was brilliantly lit and packed with television screens, curved coloured glass rectangles, each showing a different picture of distant places all over the globe and what was going on there – football matches, volcanoes erupting, yachts capsizing, people planting rice, waterfalls, great bulldozers chewing away at the desert.

'It's like a live atlas,' Simon said contentedly, leaning back in the wheelchair as Aunt Gwen pushed him homewards. She took Simon to the clinic three days a week: what was done to him there didn't seem to help, in fact it made him feel worse, but they said it was for his benefit so he supposed he must put up with it good-temperedly. In the end it would make little difference, but perhaps by then they would have learned facts that would help other people.

Simon lay back, consciously relaxing to quell the choked feeling that arose from treatment at the clinic, and looking forward to the evening. Evenings never varied: Jeff read aloud – poetry, his own or other people's – and if there was a travel film on TV they looked at it.

Simon was small and dark-haired and very calm; he liked to laugh too, and found a lot of things surprisingly funny, but few people knew that, apart from Jeff and Aunt Gwen. Simon worried sometimes about Jeff, but kept the worry to himself: only the future could untie *that* knot.

Jeff came home at six in a bad temper.

'Old Goodman says I take too long on repair jobs, doing them too carefully,' he growled, shovelling down hamburger and chips. '*He* says it doesn't pay off – all I need do is just join two ends together.'

Simon watched his skinny, active, red-haired brother nostalgically. Once he too could have eaten hamburger and chips, but not any more; thin soup or milk was his lot now, day in day out.

'You mustn't go against Mr Goodman, Jeffie,' said Aunt Gwen, all of a twitter. She was a pale wispy woman with hair in a shiny net. 'Not the way things are, with – with the rent rise and prices going up all the time. You have to do the job his way.'

'I know, I know,' said Jeff, slamming tea into his mug. Jeff's earnings had supported the family since Mr and Mrs Tichborne had been killed in a coach crash on the M5 two years ago. His college plans had to be put off, perhaps permanently, for Aunt Gwen's time was mainly spent on looking after Simon, and would be even more, quite soon.

'Goodman's full of slime – he's like an overripe puffball. One minute smarming the customers, next minute telling me to skimp on the job. And then he'll ask after Sim in that oozy sugary voice: "How's the little fellow getting on? Is he any better?" Ugh! he makes me sick!'

'What's your parrot's name?' said Sim softly, and Jeff burst into an unwilling guffaw, remembering the time last summer when Mr Goodman had come with the truck to pick him up for an emergency repair. There had been an owl on the draining-board: Jeff had found it, stunned, in Dyeworks Lane the previous evening, and Sim, who loved wild creatures and was clever with them, had dressed a wound on its wing and given it brandy. Two days later it was well enough to fly away, but in the meantime Mr Goodman, calling, had mistaken it for a parrot.

'He asked after the parrot, just last week. I said it had flown away.'

'What did he say?'

'Oh, what a shame. The little fellow ought to have a pet.'

'A nice fluffy kitten with a blue ribbon,' suggested Sim.

Then they watched a film about the Amazon, and, after it finished, Jeff read aloud his latest which was called 'Group Therapy', and Sim made some useful criticisms. Then, as he often did, Sim asked for Chidiock Tichborne's poem, and Jeff read that.

Next Sunday afternoon Sim was out in the front garden in his wheelchair, making a careful drawing of Mrs Trevor's Labrador, Sootie, who lay heaving in the sun on the next-door lawn, when Mr Goodman drove up in the truck to collect Jeff for another urgent repair job.

'That's right, that's right,' he said, giving Sim's drawing

an indulgent glance. 'Pretty good, eh?' Sim drew formidably well. 'I suppose you'd like a doggie of your own, wouldn't you? What's your favourite sort?'

'No – I don't want a dog.' Foreseeing all kinds of tiresomeness if Mr Goodman took this notion into his head, Sim added quickly and absently, 'I'd rather take a trip to Niagara.' On the grass beside him lay a library book which contained six different painters' views of the waterfall; Sim had been thinking how very nice it would be to paint his own version, and add a seventh to the total. *That* would be a thing to leave behind. Sim knew that he was due to die, not very far in the future; he had grown accustomed to the prospect and didn't particularly mind it, but there were things he wanted to do first.

'A trip to Niagara? Well I never!' said Mr Goodman, quite taken aback. For the moment he was silenced. Later in the week, though, he told Jeff, 'You ought to get your younger brother to Niagara if that's what he wants. After all, there isn't much –' He thought for a moment and added, 'Maybe the local paper would do an appeal.'

Jeff scowled without answering. He loathed the idea of charity.

'Do you really want to see Niagara so badly?' he asked Simon that evening.

'No, no; old Goodman got carried away by sentiment as usual.' Just the same, he had a distant look in his eye that troubled his brother.

Jeff had read stories in the paper about dying children who longed to go to a Butlins camp or Buckingham Palace or Southend, and kind neighbours who clubbed together to arrange the treat. He found the idea a bit sickening. Fine for the neighbours who, no doubt, felt all puffed up with virtue and kindness. But what about the children, after the treat was over, when all they had was death to wait for? Had they really been done such a good turn?

Sim was different, of course: Sim was special. He had done such a lot of thinking in his life that in some ways he seemed the older of the two brothers.

Niagara, though! That was going to cost a fortune!

Jeff began thinking about ways of earning money. Then he saw the advertisement in the local paper: GUARD WANTED.

His annual three-week holiday was due. He had intended to spend it moonlighting, freelancing on electrical repair jobs, but that would annoy Mr Goodman very much if he got to hear of it, as he undoubtedly would; and the newspaper offer was not bad pay, eighty pounds a week. Two hundred and forty pounds with what Jeff had saved up . . .

He went and inquired about the job at the office of the local Nature Conservancy Board.

'You realize it would be a non-stop watching responsibility?' said Miss Plowright, the secretary of the Board, who interviewed him. 'We have guards alternating in twelve-hour shifts. And you have to stay right there, all the time. Five minutes away from the spot, and somebody could whip in; then all of the work would have been for nothing.'

'Yes I do see that,' said Jeff, quite trembling with anxiety.

'What's your job – when you aren't doing guard work?' asked Miss Plowright, studying Jeff with curiosity. She thought he looked too thin and too angry, and perhaps too imbued with imagination for his own good – imagination that was never, or hardly ever, allowed out for an airing.

She thought of moles, burrowing in the dark, with their powerful claws: what happens to moles' claws if they are not allowed to burrow?

'I – oh, I'm a poet,' said Jeff absently. 'I mean I'm an electrician,' he added next minute, blushing with fury. He had been thinking how much he was going to enjoy sitting out all night on the grassy hillside, thinking how, for once, he would have *time* to think.

'A poet? Or an electrician?' Miss Plowright smiled slowly. 'Nothing to stop you being both.'

'Well I had an ancestor who was a poet. At least, he wrote one poem.'

Now why had he told the woman that? But she did not seem at all surprised; perhaps people often told her things.

'Tichborne, Tichborne,' she murmured. 'I know that name. Didn't he plot against the queen? And write a very sad poem on the eve of his execution?'

'He was a Catholic, you see. He was only twenty-eight when they executed him.'

> 'My tale was heard, and yet it was not told
> My fruit is fallen, yet my leaves are green –'

'That's the one.'

'He is certainly an ancestor to put you on your mettle,' said Miss Plowright. 'I can see it will be a job to live up to him.'

Jeff thought, recklessly, of telling her that they had yet another ancestor, Elspeth Tichborne, accused of witchcraft and burned at the stake, leaving, with her dying breath, such a curse on the judges who condemned her that all three died of the plague the following year. But he did not, and later was glad that he had not.

Miss Plowright was going on thoughtfully, 'I can quite see why this kind of job had an appeal for you. What kind of poet are you?' And, as he looked blank, 'Traditional or otherwise?'

'Oh, traditional.'

'Regular metre? Rhyme?'

'Yes.'

'Hmm, that's a pity.'

'Why?'

'You might be so occupied trying to think of a rhyme that you would let the thieves get past you.'

'I would not!' said Jeff, stung. Later he was to remember that too.

'All right, all right, I trust you!' she said. 'And the job's yours. Night shift. I must say I do prefer rhyming poetry myself. Now, I'll tell you where to find the site. Here's a large-scale map. And don't, please, *don't* breathe a word to a single soul, not your nearest and dearest, *nobody*. This job is no joke, you know, it's deadly serious. We aren't paying out a hundred and sixty pounds a week just for fun.'

'Not a single soul,' promised Jeff, wondering how he was going to explain his night-time activities to Sim and Aunt Gwen.

But Miss Plowright said, 'Of course, you can tell them that you are guarding a plant. But not just what and where. Or – seriously – you might be followed.'

'It's like a spy story.'

'It's almost worse. The things that selfish, greedy, uncaring people will do for money: or for rare specimens. In spite of the fact that there would be a fine of a thousand pounds for each plant stolen – very likely a prison sentence too. It's an endangered species, you see; there are only two known sites where it grows in England. Sad, really: when your ancestor wrote his poem there might have been hundreds of them, scattered all over the Downs. But, with ploughing, and herbicides and ignorant people who pick them –'

'And greedy, *un*-ignorant people who dig them up –'

'Yes, and of course they are also subject to the ordinary risks that affect any plant – they may be trodden on by cows, or nibbled by rabbits or flattened by motorbike scramblers ...

Well, there you have it. Enjoy your watching. Recite your ancestor's poem, if you can't think up one of your own, and *keep awake*.'

Mr Goodman dropped in, one evening during Jeff's three-week leave.

'I know the lad's on holiday, but I thought as I knew he wasn't going away . . . and I reckoned he'd be pleased to pick up a bit of extra cash –'

It was another urgent repair job.

'I'm afraid my nephew's not here,' said Aunt Gwen, flustered.

'Ah? Out enjoying himself, is he? Don't blame him.'

Sim thought dispassionately that Mr Goodman's round pink face, with the little deep-sunk eyes like sparks, was like a fruit that has begun to decay, a soggy tomato with the stem sinking into a tiny wrinkled pit, and the flesh under the skin turning soft and rotten. For some obscure reason the look of it recalled great-great-great-grandmother Elspeth's curse: 'I curse the lips that spake the sentence and the hard hearts that ordained it; I curse the hands that writ the accusation and the bodies that bore them; may they rot before the grave, and die before death take them, and roast in hell-fire eternally thereafter . . .'

'No – no, he's out on a job,' twittered Aunt Gwen. 'To earn enough to send Simmie here away on a trip –'

Sim heaved a resigned sigh.

Mr Goodman said, 'Niagara! yes, yes of course! And a grand sight it'll be, young man, when you get there, it will indeed. Repair job?' probed Mr Goodman sharply and delicately. 'Not going behind my back to any of my customers, I hope?'

'No, no, of course not, not a repair job. Watching over a plant –'

Sim looked gravely at Aunt Gwen, who bit her lip and shut up. But Mr Goodman went right on probing.

'A plant, eh? That's interesting! One of those rare ones the World Wildlife folk are so hot on preserving? Funny, isn't it, really, they should spend so much on that when there's so much money wanted for other things – research on illness – like the lad here, and people dying of starvation in Africa and all the homeless . . . Mind you, I'm keen on plants meself, got a nice few lilies and tropical orchids in my little greenhouse, they've no better specimens at Kew though I do say so – but you've got to have a sense of proportion, haven't you? Would it be an orchid, then, the boy's minding?'

'I can't say,' said Aunt Gwen faintly. 'He never told us.'

'Very right, very right. Very right. Can't trust anybody, these days. Maybe it'd be one of those monkey orchids, it's said they grow round here, up on Tillingham Down. *Very* uncommon, those are – there's a few more over in Berkshire, and that's all they know of. You'd like to see them, I daresay, wouldn't you, young man? You could make one of your drawings of them, maybe?'

'I'm not very good at drawing plants,' Sim said politely.

'No? Well, I mustn't stand here with the grass growing under my feet . . .'

Mr Goodman trotted out, his pink face shining, paused for a word with Mrs Trevor in her garden next door, who nodded and pointed to the right; then he shot off in his repair truck with the electric flashes in gold and green and Goodman's Lightning Service blazoned along the side.

The first week passed quickly, and the second.

There was, of course, an easy way up on to Tillingham

Down: first the road until you came to Gamekeeper's Cottages, then across a farmyard past three silos, along by a wheatfield and up a chalk track beside a beechwood. But, in order to foil possible observers, Jeff and his co-watcher, a dour chemistry student called Pat Jones from Leeds, adopted various roundabout routes to the site, scrambling up the side of the hill through the steep hanging woods, or right round to the back and across the racecourse, or up the Roman road two miles away eastwards and so along the top of the ridge. Jeff began to know the little patch of woodland and the clearing where the orchid grew as well as his own front garden.

And the flowers? They were strange little twisted knots at the top of pale three-inch stems, tiny things, too unimportant-looking to be deemed worthy of so much care and surveillance. They were withered, the flowering-time was past – that was in May of course – and seed-pods were already forming; but Miss Plowright had shown Jeff pictures, and then he had looked them up himself at home in the *Concise British Flora*. They were a purplish, reddish colour, had two tiny legs, two tiny arms, a tail, a head with an infinitesimal darkish face – malevolent – two dots of green eyes and a kind of bishop's mitre, three-pointed, in a lighter pink matching the pale pink stomach. A monkey bishop! Strangely enough, the little monkey-faces in the picture had a definite look of young Sim – there was something of his perky, detached quality in the way they stood springily on their stalks.

Jeff had grown to be very fond of them; he had a fatherly, protective attitude towards the withered little entities, waiting so mildly for their seed-time and the end of summer. Here they had grown, here they waited, in this same hollow of downland, perhaps for hundreds of years, while kings came to the throne and went, while wars were fought, while

24

Chidiock Tichborne wrote his poem and waited for the executioner, while great-great-great-grandmother reviled the bishops and judges, swore that she was innocent of the charges they laid against her and then went up in flames.

Why are people so horrible to each other? Jeff wondered, sitting in the quiet dewy woods which were never completely silent at night, and never quite dark. The sky, crammed with stars, hung low over the trees; then, long before sunrise, the stars faded and the sky brightened. Always, somewhere, there was something in motion – a twig snapping or a fan of leaves rustling. At first Jeff was nervous of these noises, expected wolves or bandits or boa constrictors, he hardly knew what. But soon he became accustomed to the sounds: they were just the night creatures of the woods, going about their business.

But why *are* people so horrible? They were no worse, those people in bygone days, than we are now. We are no more civilized than they were, we shoot and fight each other on the least excuse, we grab and steal what is not ours. Take the people who are after this little orchid. Why can't they leave it to grow in peace? How can somebody who has enough specialized knowledge to be aware of its value still be so callously selfish? You'd think that orchid hunters would be a cut above other collectors, but no, they are just as greedy and ruthless, just as ready to break laws and do irreparable damage.

A plaguing mischief light on ye, hateful brigands! Elspeth Tichborne had shouted, as they tied her to the stake. My curse on the lot of ye! May the sun never warm ye, nor water quench your thirst. May the seeds shrivel that ye plant, and the food turn to gall in your bellies. I am innocent, and shall declare it to the last.

But they had burned her just the same.

In the third week, Sim caught a cold. This was serious, for Sim had no resistance at all to germs, any bacillus that floated by could knock him endways. From germs at the clinic, of course, it was impossible to protect him, and Jeff privately thought that the clinic was the source of many of their problems; but this time it was indubitably Mr Goodman, who dropped in one teatime to inquire if Jeff would be free to come and rewire a church hall that evening.

'What? Still going off on those late-night outings? *We* know what to think when a young feller is out all night for weeks on end, don't we, Miss Tichborne?' With a wink. 'Oh, I know, I know, he says he's watching over the monkey orchid – but we know better than that, don't we?'

'I never said anything about what I was doing,' corrected Jeff.

'Nor you did! Nor you did. Just me going on. Why, if you were doing that, you'd not have to worry about raising cash to send the laddie to Niagara. They say there's collectors who'd pay thousands for a single seed pod.'

Mr Goodman fixed Jeff with an eye like a laser beam.

'Of *course* an honest young feller-me-lad like you, that does his work so carefully, would never pay any heed to types like that. HECK-tishooooo!' He gave a tremendous sneeze. 'Got a bit of a cold, been out late too many nights meself – doing your work for you, young Jeff.'

Squawking remonstrance, Aunt Gwen almost pushed Mr Goodman out of the kitchen. But the mischief was done: next day Sim was reduced to a limp flop of gasping misery, needed non-stop nursing and an oxygen cylinder in his room.

It was after three days of this, helping Aunt Gwen nurse by day, watching by night, that Jeff one night fell asleep under his hawthorn spinney, while trying to think of a rhyme for silver.

When he awoke, in the dripping hush of a grey and sodden dawn, the seed heads were gone. The monkey orchid stems had been clipped, very neatly, with scissors, close to the base.

For about ten minutes Jeff was numb with shock. He sat staring at the patch of ground: he literally found it impossible to believe his eyes. But there were the thirteen raw little stumps, and a couple of dark, bruised footprints in the rain-soaked turf. He found a crushed hollow in a nearby bramble-clamp, where somebody had stood and waited. Jeff detested the thought of that, almost more than all else: that a person, his enemy, had stood there, watching, studying him, perhaps for several nights, waiting to pounce on the single moment of oblivion. And at last it had come. And Jeff had failed in his task. And the seed heads were gone.

'They weren't even mature,' mourned Miss Plowright. 'They weren't ripe, and now the seeds won't germinate. He won't get any good out of them – whoever he is.'

'I didn't tell anybody. I never even said the name.' Jeff wished he were dead and underground. Miss Plowright looked at him sadly. He couldn't bear the look in her eyes. Perhaps she believed he had taken them? Had sold them?

'I'm sure you didn't,' she said. 'The fact that someone knew where they were need not be your fault at all. These things get around.'

'It's my fault they were stolen,' said Jeff. '*I* fell asleep.' Wretchedly he stared back at Miss Plowright, with eyes full of tears. And she had no comfort to offer him.

'She did offer me the pay, but of course I wouldn't take it,' he told Aunt Gwen later.

'*Course* you couldn't,' croaked Sim, who, mercifully, was a little better that morning, off the oxygen and even able to drink some orange juice from a cup.

27

Then Sim added thoughtfully, 'I'm going to put great-great-great-grandma's curse on whoever took the monkey orchid. Maybe that'll protect all the other specimens, too.'

'Don't try to talk, child, you'll tire yourself,' warned Aunt Gwen, carrying a bowl and towel out of the room. But Jeff could see that the idea of the curse was a distraction from his own misery and discomfort.

Sim went on slowly, 'I bet if great-granny Elspeth had been in charge of the orchids, she'd have set a guardian by them.'

'What sort of guardian?' asked Jeff, humouring him.

'Like a great black shaggy monkey – but shapeless and soggy, with cold arms, ice-cold hands and feet that would grab you and hold you tight to its soggy chest. And it would puff into your face with its cold stinking breath – like the smell from a dustbin. It would feel like all the hate in the world, come to grab you: hate that's been piling up for hundreds of years.'

'Don't!' said Jeff with a shiver. Sim's words somehow embodied the very thought he had had in his own mind; he could feel the awful black thing take shape and expand, like a heaving black balloon, out there, or in there –

To distract himself from the thought he said, 'I'm sorry, I'm really sorry about Niagara, Simmie.'

'Oh, that's all right. Niagara doesn't matter a bit,' Sim said absently. 'I don't suppose I'd have been able to draw it, anyway. Why don't you collect me a lot of those beer-can tops, the ones with loops and rings? I've got an awfully good idea for making a pattern.'

Mr Goodman was extremely shocked when he heard, after Jeff had gone back to work, that the two hundred and forty pounds had not been paid and the Niagara trip was off.

'No! Well I never! What a blessed shame! I'm *surprised* at those people. After all, you did the watching, quite OK, for two and a half weeks, you ought to have been paid for *that*. They might at least have paid you two hundred – or two-twenty.' He seemed really outraged, and paid no heed when Jeff said he wouldn't have accepted the money anyway. 'I hate for that poor mite of a lad to be disappointed, when he's got nothing else to look forward to.'

Mr Goodman worked for a while in silence, sorting invoices. He seemed to be turning Sim's condition over in his mind, perhaps comparing it to his own – today, for some reason, he seemed particularly pink and pleased with himself. He said, 'Business isn't bad, I've had one or two strokes of luck lately, maybe I could see my way to a bit of a donation –'

Jeff stared at him in horror. He muttered, 'Oh, no, that wouldn't –' and then found he couldn't bear to stay in Mr Goodman's presence a moment longer. There was something about those pink cheeks, those bright little eyes, those big clever fingers so handy with pliers or screwdriver, that made him feel sick. He bolted out saying something about a thermostat.

But late that evening, when Jeff arrived home through thundery rain, he found Mr Goodman there already with Aunt Gwen, making his offer. 'I'll be only too glad to pay the lad's fare, if that's what he's set his heart on. In fact I've a cheque already written –'

'But it's not what I've set my heart on, Mr Goodman,' whispered Sim. 'I don't feel quite up to drawing Niagara. Instead I'm planning a picture of my great-great-great-grandmother's curse. D'you want to hear about it, Mr Goodman? She put it on the people who did her harm. It looks like a gathering – a great poisoned swelling in the shape of a monkey that will grow inside a person, inside the thief who stole the flowers that Jeff was looking after. Soon, very soon, it will burst out of that person, like a seed out of a pod –'

'*Don't* Sim!' cried out Jeff. 'You mustn't!'

But Mr Goodman, without waiting for Sim to finish, had run out of the room and out of the house. A jag of lightning greeted him, and a flurry of rain: summer was breaking up fast.

'What in the world ails the man?' demanded Aunt Gwen, coming in with a cup of milk. 'Was he taken ill? He looked terrible.'

'He's afraid of illness,' Sim said calmly. 'Did you remember to bring me any beer-can tops, Jeff?'

'I did find half a dozen.' Jeff looked dazed. Slowly he emptied his pockets. 'Here ...' He was thinking about the monkey: the black, wet, heavy, hating monkey. Gradually, by slow degrees, it lifted itself away from him and drifted away, after Mr Goodman, into the outside world. Let it go! Let it never come back! 'Here they are,' he said, and arranged the can tops on Sim's bedside table.

Sim, still too weak to make a drawing of them, lay back on his pillow and looked them over with great content.

'They'll do nicely,' he said.

The two brothers rested in silence until Sim sighed and murmured, 'Say Chidiock's poem. Say it all through.'

> 'My prime of youth is but a frost of cares
> My feast of joy is but a dish of pain
> My crop of corn is but a field of tares
> And all my good is but vain hope of gain.
> The day is past and yet I saw no sun
> And now I live and now my life is done.'

Jeff said the other two verses as well.

'It's very good,' Sim mumbled. 'Listen to how those words plod along, like a slow march. Like a person walking through mud. But you'll write one as good, by and by. Did you finish the one you were working on last night?'

'No. I stuck on a rhyme for silver.'

'You'll finish it some time,' said Sim.

Jeff was out of a job, after Mr Goodman's unexpected death, but Miss Plowright offered him one.

'Would you trust me?' he said.

'Of course I would! I could see how dreadfully upset you were about those seeds. And there are lots of things you can do for us if you care to learn a bit about plants. Perhaps you could go to evening classes.'

'I'd like to do that,' said Jeff. 'Later.'

Miss Plowright, who had come to the Tichbornes' house, understood him perfectly.

'Of course, later. I believe your brother is handy with wild creatures? I've got a hedgehog here that was found on the Canterbury road – we've mended its leg, but it needs a place to convalesce for a few days. Do you think – your garden –?'

Sim smiled gently at Miss Plowright. They seemed to have made friends without even having exchanged a single word.

Ben in Paradise

K. M. PEYTON

BEN was a bit stupid, after all.

'I don't know why you play with the boy. He's so stupid.'

Ben did not know exactly what they meant. Nobody ever told him anything. His mother never had the time to talk to him. She was always in a great lather of coming and going and being late, cooking, cleaning and looking after the six of them. She was on the buses. The others were much older than Ben, and out on the streets so fast he couldn't keep up with them.

That's why he went to Amanda's where it was quiet and slow, and Amanda's mother said in her uppity voice, 'I don't know why you play with the boy. He's so stupid.' Then she used to add, 'But he can't help it, I suppose.'

In spite of her disapproval, Ben stayed. In his experience a quiet place was rare and not to be given up readily.

'He needs God's help,' said Amanda's father.

'Yes. Well . . .' said Amanda's mother.

'I'll help him,' said Amanda, who was a goody-goody girl.

Her parents went to church. Amanda wanted to take Ben but Amanda's mother said he was too dirty.

'I'll teach him then. I'll teach him about God,' said Amanda.

'What's God?' asked Ben.

'God lives in Paradise.'

Ben knew all the bus routes because of his mother but had never heard of Paradise. Presumably it was a place beyond the reach of London Transport. Perhaps on the Green Line.

He waited to hear more.

Amanda showed him one of her holy pictures of a man in a sort of loose shirt with a white beard, surrounded by beautiful trees and grass and flowers, and a sort of light coming out of his head.

'That's God,' said Amanda.

He looked nice. Ben considered. 'He's not in London then?'

'God is everywhere,' said Amanda mysteriously.

She looked at Ben with a sigh and said kindly, 'God loves you. He loves black and white equally.'

That would surprise Kev, Ben thought, and Kev's friends, who always complained of being picked on.

'He loves animals too, and flowers, and everything.'

Ben went home and said all this to Kev, who said, 'Your blankety God doesn't love you much, else he wouldn't have made you so blankety stupid, would 'e?'

'Don't talk to him like that! He can't help it,' said his mum, and went out to work.

Ben went out too, because Kev and Trev and Mo and Joe and Moxy were all in the kitchen playing tapes and his head ached. He was thinking about God who loved everybody and wondering how he might get in with God, like Amanda. Apart from when God was in Paradise, his London home seemed to be in church, from what Amanda said, but when Ben looked in he got chased out by an old woman cleaning the floor.

'We don't want you messing about in God's house, you dirty little heathen!' said God's cleaner. 'Get out of here, footprints all over my floor!'

'Is God very clean?' Ben asked Amanda.

'He said is God very clean?' Amanda repeated to her mother, laughing.

'Poor little soul,' said Amanda's mother, who was the cleanest person Ben had ever seen.

Then she said to Ben, 'It doesn't matter. God loves the very lowest.'

Ben reckoned that counted him in.

'How do I find God then?'

'You find God in church.'

'No.' Only the cleaning woman.

'Mind you, I draw the line at taking him to church,' said Amanda's mother. 'I'll do most things for the cause, but take that child to church on a Sunday and have him sit with us is more than I will do for God.'

'You do cream teas for Jesus very nicely, dear,' said Amanda's father. 'That's enough.'

'Who's Jesus?'

'Jesus is the son of God,' said Amanda.

Ben had to reconsider. This put God in a new light: a family man.

'He lives with him?'

34

'No. He's gone out into the world.'

'He's got a job then?'

'Sort of, yes.'

'He's on the dole?'

'No. Jesus isn't on the dole.' Amanda went into peals of laughter.

Ben couldn't get a clear picture at all, every question he asked seeming to produce mirth and confusion. But as this was the effect he often had on people, he didn't take it badly.

Finding God in church having proved a non-starter, Ben decided to keep his eyes open for Paradise. Amanda said it was a beautiful place with grass and trees and flowers. There was only one place Ben knew where there was grass and trees and flowers, and that was a patch of land where there had once been an old house. The house had been demolished and the old garden had grown very wild. There was a factory on one side and some boarded-up houses on the other.

He went to have a look. There was a drive in through a narrow gateway. The drive curved round through the overgrown shrubs to a yard at the back, once a stable block and coach-house, now as dilapidated as the house and garden around it. Outside the building a flat pony-cart stood, the sort scrap men still used. It had an old washing-machine on it, and scattered around the yard were articles of scrap – an old pram, a bedstead or two, a filing cabinet and a tangled heap of rusty wire-netting. Ben looked around doubtfully.

As he did so an old man appeared in the doorway of the building. He had a white beard and wore a shirt like in Amanda's picture, and held a fork in his hand with a sausage on it.

Ben was confused.

'Is this Paradise?'

35

The man laughed. 'Yeah, mate. I reckon it is. Welcome to Paradise.'

After the cleaning lady in the church, Ben felt much encouraged. The sausage didn't seem right somehow, but the rest fitted. The man went inside again and Ben followed. The old stable was mostly full of junk but there were two ponies in the stalls, a black one and a white one, and in a little room at one end, where once the harness had been kept, the man with the white beard was cooking over an old-fashioned grate. He was just tipping a tin of baked beans into a frying pan where three sausages were already sizzling and well-burnt. A very old dog lay in front of the fire asleep; the ponies were munching steadily, and there was an aura of peaceful domesticity that Ben had never come across before, certainly not at home, and not at Amanda's either. This, more than anything, attracted him.

To test him, Ben asked the man, 'Which do you love best? The black one or the white one?'

'Come again?'

Ben pointed towards the ponies.

The man laughed. 'Why, they're both the same to me, mate.' He gave the pan a stir round. 'Want a sausage?'

Ben reckoned the man was God.

God gave him the sausage and said, 'Poor little blighter. Where d'you live, mate?'

'Anstey Court.'

'Your ma know where you are?'

He shook his head.

'Have this sausage and cut along then. We don't want her worried.'

Ben didn't understand. His ma never worried. Not about him, at least; only about money for the gas meter or fags or being late for work.

He sat down with the sausage by the dog and started to eat. The dog got up, interested in the smell of food, and God gave him a sausage of his own. He lay down again by Ben with the sausage between his paws. He was a black mongrel with sad, faded eyes. He smelt rather. Ben liked him.

'What's his name?'

'Blackie – like you, mate.' God laughed.

The dog ate his sausage very slowly, holding it down with one paw and licking it a lot.

'It's 'is teeth,' said God.

He started to eat the beans out of the frying pan with a spoon, and offered a few mouthfuls to Ben. They were greasy and spitting hot.

'You live here?' Ben asked, wanting to get it right.

'While I can. I live anywhere.'

That fitted. Everywhere, Amanda had said.

'I move around like.'

'It's nice here.'

'You're right. Like you said, it's Paradise.'

All the same, like the cleaning lady, God made him go, after the beans.

'Can I come back?'

God hesitated. 'If your ma knows where you are, s'all right by me. Just drop in, like.'

But his ma wasn't interested in where he'd been. When Ben said he'd been to Paradise, she just laughed and said, 'Lucky for some!'

'I'm going again. God said I could.'

'Bully for you!' His ma drew on her cigarette with her quick, nervous movements. 'It's that Amanda, got 'im like this,' she said to Moxy.

'Funny, him being how 'e is.'

'He's no trouble.'

Ben went back to Paradise the next afternoon, but only the black pony was there. It was standing dozing, tied up in its stall. It looked rather old to Ben, like the dog. Ben went and sat down in front of it, and the pony put its head down and blew hot breath over Ben's cold hands. Its muzzle was very soft, like moss. Ben liked it. He stayed there until God came home. It had gone dark, and was raining, and God got a fright when Ben stood up.

'Mate! 'Strewth!'

He had the white pony with him, which he led into its stall. The old dog went to the empty grate and lay down on its sack in front of the ashes. God brought some wood in off the cart and lit the fire. He lit a pressure lantern and hung it from the hook in the ceiling, and opened a large tin of baked beans and shook them into the frying pan.

'You feed the ponies, eh, mate? Give 'em some hay.'

'What's hay?'

'That stuff at the end. That old grass, mate. Put some under their noses.'

He stepped over the dog to settle the bean pan over the fire. 'Pity you don't eat hay, mate,' he said to the dog. 'You might do better.'

The flames danced and made patterns over the ceiling. Ben sat and shared God's beans. God made him stay till it stopped raining. The ponies munched the hay with a monotonous, rhythmic grinding of jaws and the mongrel licked himself very slowly, with lots of sighs and groans and rootlings round and round on the sack.

'You gotta go home, mate.'

'I like it here.'

'Yeah. Well. You told your ma?'

'Yes. I told her.'

God shook his head. He made some tea in an enamel jug,

very strong, and gave Ben a mugful, with lots of sugar and condensed milk. It was wonderful.

'Can I come again?'

'Yeah, mate. You can come when you like.'

Ben learned about feeding the ponies, and making a fire in the grate. God took the ponies turn and turn about, one day on, one day off. They were both old, he said, like the dog, like himself. 'We gotta look after ourselves. Slow but steady.' The dog rode on the cart and barked if anyone came near. He never barked off the cart, God said.

'He'll die soon, like me. He's eighteen. That's a hundred and twenty-six if he was human. That's old, mate.'

God sighed.

'You – you're just starting.' He paused, considering Ben. 'You never got a fair crack of the whip right from the start, did you, mate? What's going to become of you, I wonder?'

He made Ben a cup of tea. Ben watched the thick milk slide over the lip of the tin and down into the mug, trembling to the shake of God's hand. Paradise indeed! He trembled too, with love for God and Paradise. No one had ever been good to him as God was good to him.

But God said, 'We gotta go soon, mate. You know that?'

'Where to?'

God shrugged. 'Move on. Anywhere we can find. They're coming in here with the bulldozer. Make a block of flats, that's what. They're going to flatten this lot.'

But Ben only thought of the here and now.

'No,' he said.

God laughed. 'Yes, mate! That's life. That's how it goes.'

Ben went every day and ate beans and sausages and fed the ponies. The dog wagged its tail when he came in. Ben took him half a hamburger he found in a dustbin. The dog lay with its paws on it and licked it slowly and Ben knew he was pleased.

The next day he went there was a bulldozer in the garden. Where the stable had been was just a pile of bricks and a pile of timber. The cart had gone, and the ponies and the dog, and God. Even the washing-machine and the rusty wire and the old pram. A young man was putting an old motor tyre on the pile of timber, to set light to it. Ben stood and looked.

The young man laughed at him.

'What *you* want, dummy?'

Ben did not answer. He had known, even before the young man had spoken, exactly what he was going to say. It was like old times, before Paradise. He turned round and went home.

Dancing Bear

JOHN CHRISTOPHER

I

THE news of the fall of the City came on my thirteenth birthday. After a summer mostly of rain and grumbling storm, the weather had cleared. Waking early, I looked out from my small window high up in the palace wall to see men trudging through mist towards the cornfields. They toiled there as the sun scorched upwards, reaping and stacking and binding. At midday I went out with the kitchen girls who took them bread and cheese and pots of ale. When they had eaten and drunk they lay in the hedgerow's shade, enjoying the brief rest that was permitted. I had been with them in the fields hundreds of times before, but this was the first time I was truly aware of them as peasants, men who must labour their lives away at another's command. I looked at

41

Wyngraeth, snoring beneath a hawthorn tree. He was taller and broader even than my father; but he touched his forelock to the gentry, and today had done so to me.

My presents were not given me until the evening feast. The horse first – a groom led it into the hall, and my father called me up to take the rein. It was nothing like the horses my father and my brother rode: a beast of the native strain, less than fourteen hands high, with little in the way either of looks or breeding. In colour it was chestnut, its mane a lighter shade, yellow almost. But it was mine. I thanked my father, bending the knee.

'How will you name him?' he said.

'Lion,' I said, staring at his tawny mane.

My brother laughed. 'So a bear will ride a lion! A sight to wonder at.'

My name is Ursus, meaning bear.

My father said, 'It is a gift which demands a second.'

He beckoned to his steward, who came forward to present a sword, hilt first, to my father; he in turn held the point towards his chest as he offered it to me.

'Your lion needs protecting, as all things do – by this, and your right arm.'

It was less than a man's sword as Lion was less than a man's horse, but I would exchange both for better as I grew. This time I knelt. He raised me up and called for wine to drink the health of this his son, a boy no longer.

The feast had begun at the ninth hour. It was well past the eleventh; lamps had been lit and outside the day was fading. Eating had moderated, from fullness, but drinking had not, though now they were supping ale: wine, in this chill province, was too precious to be wasted even at a birthday feast.

Nearly all the men were marked by liquor, and my

brother, Primus, was plainly drunk, his speech slurred and his movements slow and awkward. When our father went outside to relieve himself, he baited me, giving rein to the animosity which he concealed in his presence. Flavius Rufus, my father's Master of Soldiers and trusted friend, had gone with him: I was surrounded by my brother's cronies. Servants heaped logs on the fire, and I jumped when a spark flew out and burnt my hand. Primus laughed, and seized a brand from the edge of the blaze. He jabbed the burning end, like a dagger, at my feet.

'Is our little bear afraid of fire?' he asked. 'Well, then, he must learn to dance. Come, dancing bear, show us how you can jig!'

Although we shared a father, we had different mothers. His had been divorced to make way for mine, and had gone – some said been forced – to live with an order of religious women a day's ride from the court. Even after my mother died, when I was four years old, she did not return. I could not recall a time when he had not tormented me in private: it was something I had learned to endure. But this was in public, at my birthday feast, where I had been given a horse and a sword. I stared at him, not flinching when the brand's end seared my naked leg. Through long painful moments our gazes locked, until with another laugh he tossed the stick back on to the fire.

'The day will come when you *will* dance, little bear, and to my tune. I promise that.'

The messenger arrived when night had already fallen: the ship had docked towards dusk and in the excitement of the feasting no one, not even any of the servants, had looked down to the harbour to see it. He was known to us all, having served many years as an imperial courier, a taciturn, solemn man with a wife and children in the village. He bowed to my father, and offered him the scroll from his pouch. But as my father broke the seal, he said:

'There is later news than is written down, Illustrious.'

My father stared at him. He too had drunk deeply, but showed nothing. He said sharply, 'What news?'

The courier hesitated; in his face there was a heaviness that differed from the melancholy which was natural to him.

'Tell it, man!'

He did, and we heard him in a stillness which was like the stillness in church before the bell rings to mark the elevation of the Host; except that this stillness was not of expectancy but incredulity and dread.

Once a week my father held a council of government. It was attended by his senior officers: the Master of Soldiers, the Officer of Laws and the Procurator of Finance. Also by the Governor's son – following my recent birthday by both his sons. Our presence was irregular, but we lived in irregular times. Nor, if a complaint were to be made, was there a place to which it could be addressed, now the City had fallen.

It was of this my father spoke. Further word had come to confirm the courier's story. This time the barbarians had not been content with camping outside the walls until gold was brought to send them on their way. Treacherously a gate had been opened – by barbarian slaves, it was said – and they had stormed through it and taken what they liked, stripping gold from holy ornaments, rings from women's fingers, plundering and burning, raping and slaughtering and defiling. This had continued for three days, before they took their booty and withdrew.

'It is hard and ugly news,' my father said. He looked older, I thought, and there was greyness in his face. 'But the empire has been through dangerous times before.'

44

He paused, but no one spoke. I would not have presumed to, but the silence of the rest signified much: dangerous times, maybe, but it was the City itself whose might had been the means of weathering them.

'And in the east the empire is still strong. For the moment we are separated from our friends by the barbarians, but the division will not last. When the time is ripe the emperor will launch the counter-stroke which will send them scuttling back to their stinking dens. Meanwhile, our best duty is to uphold ancient customs and traditions. While they live, the empire lives. Our ancestors conquered this land, and gave civilization to its people. What they won, we must hold and preserve. We have barbarians of our own, close at hand. We had better look to them.'

The greyness of my father's face marked more than a lowness of spirit. He was stricken by an agony in the belly which in the end he could not conceal. His strength waned with the summer, and the flesh seemed to melt from his bones. In early winter, I stood at my brother's side by the grave into which his coffin was to be lowered, his feet towards the east. On the coffin rested a heavy gold torque, the tributary gift, more than a century ago, of a local king to the governor of this province. A gaudy ornament, my father had said, but the toga dignified it; and it impressed the natives. It was part of the imperial regalia, which would pass to his successor.

His will was read next day at the funeral feast. He left legacies to the church, and to friends; but the bulk of his estate was to be divided between my brother and myself, in equal parts. I listened, half hearing, and left the feast soon after. Flavius Rufus discovered me in the stables.

He said, 'A successor to your father must be found. No, listen, Ursus – this is important. The appointment should

45

come from the Senate, but even if there is still a Senate we have no way of making known our needs, nor they of answering them. Normally, as Master of Soldiers, I would hold office until a replacement was named. But there can be no waiting now. The council tomorrow will do its own naming, and will name your brother.'

'Why him?' I asked. 'Why not you?'

'Because there are discords you do not know of. The barbarians threaten too, and will soon move against us. I have no great liking for your brother, but under him, your father's son, maybe we can unite. It is our only hope.'

He paused, looking at me. His red hair was chiefly grey now, and sparse. He said, 'Our hope, but not yours. You will not live to get your legacy, if you stay. But you will be safe at the abbey, providing you put on the cloth.'

I stared, shocked and angry. 'Become a priest? I will take my chance here.'

'You have no chance here. And vows can be dispensed. No man survives as a soldier without learning the difference between courage and foolhardiness.' He took a pouch from his tunic. 'Give this to the Abbot. Ride now, and fast.'

The abbey stood on high ground, twenty miles to the east. Its church was still being built but already was larger than the Governor's palace. The main part was completed: the entrance and atrium, the long nave with columned aisles, the apse with the main altar, and the chapel to Our Lady on the north side of the apse. Men laboured on the Joseph chapel that faced it.

Abbot Marcus was small of stature, meagre looking, modest in demeanour. He was surprised to see me, knowing the funeral feast would be still in progress, but welcoming at first. Then, when he discovered the reason for my being there, he was alarmed. He was a man anxious to avoid trouble, and could not conceal his misgiving.

Despising him, I said, 'You have the message from Flavius Rufus. I am to be an acolyte, and then a priest. Will you accept me, Lord Abbot?'

Looking at him I knew he would dearly have loved to say no, but refusal could lead to trouble as surely as acceptance: he feared to offend the Master of Soldiers as much as he feared my brother's wrath. For my part, I did not care if it was yea or nay. I would not go back – I had considered what Flavius Rufus had said, and though young was not a fool – but these were times which would furnish employment for anyone – a lad, even – who had a horse and sword.

He said, in his soft frail voice, 'The church offers sanctuary to all who seek it. You may stay.'

I nodded. 'Thank you, Lord Abbot. I will attend to the stabling of my horse.'

'Others will do that.'

I shook my head, 'It is mine, and I will see to it.'

He looked at me with a harder eye. 'No. You have nothing now: all is the Lord's.' His eye went to the sword that hung from my belt, and he put out a hand. 'That, too. We use no weapons here.'

A day earlier I might have turned angrily away, but I was learning. A horse, my father had said, was nothing without a sword, and a sword was meaningless without a right arm to wield it. I would yield up the first two, for the time being. The third would get them back, when the time was ripe.

For several days I hourly waited the arrival of some messenger from the court, perhaps of my brother in person with his cronies, and laid plans to escape. I knew of the inviolability of holy sanctuary but had little faith in the Abbot's

47

resolution to uphold it. But nothing happened, and gradually I came to feel more secure. Flavius Rufus, I guessed, had told the tale well. And there would be nearer and more powerful challenges my brother would have to meet. A novice in the abbey could wait his turn.

Though eventually, of course, that turn must come. I had found where the sword I had given up had been put, at the back of a cupboard full of old vestments and religious vessels, and in the time I had to myself I practised using it. In fact I was left on my own a great deal. The priests and the other acolytes took their cue from the Abbot: they spoke little to me, and required of me still less. It was plain I was an embarrassment, which they hoped would pass. I was not even tonsured until I asked for it. I did not think a shaven head would prevent my brother from killing me, but in the presence of others it might hold him back.

I attended at the Mass, of course, and as days turned into weeks came to know the church as I had known my father's palace. It was a pleasant building, full of the holy scent which is made from frankincense and myrrh, those gifts the Wise Men brought to the infant Jesus. And that third gift which they brought was there in plenty, too. Gold dishes, gold bowls for holy water and gold ewers for the sacred wine, a gold monstrance studded with gems to contain the host, a gold and ivory staff which the Abbot carried in procession . . . When they were not in use they were kept in a chest in the Lady chapel. And in a smaller chest, high up on the wall, was the greatest treasure of all: the dish from which, it was said, Our Lord and His disciples supped at the Passover feast. Its sacredness was such that it was never displayed to the laity, and only shown to the clergy at the Easter Mass. I was curious to see it, but Easter was more than half a year away, and the thought of still being here then gave me no joy.

And yet there seemed small prospect of anything happening to take me away. I had hoped to get word from Flavius Rufus, to hear perhaps that he had found me some other less tedious sanctuary, but no word came.

What came instead were the barbarians. Rumour preceded, of towns stormed and sacked – at first a hundred miles away, then fifty, then closer. A pedlar told a tale that my brother had taken his army against them. It was followed by report of a great victory, greeted in the abbey with excitement and relief and prayers of thankfulness. Next day we had different news – of bloody defeat and a rabble of soldiers straggling home. There were more prayers, this time of supplication. And the day after that the fur-clad long-haired savages, swinging huge axes as they marched, were on us.

The abbey was in turmoil. I looked for some sign of a defence being organized, but found none. The monks buzzed about like bees without a queen. I remembered the words of Flavius Rufus: defiance under such circumstances would be a proof not of courage but foolhardiness. I took my sword up the mountain behind the church, to a cave I knew, where the entrance was largely concealed by an ancient tree. Its roof was low; I squatted there, and listened to the sounds – the roars of bloodthirsty exultation and the answering screams – that were carried to me on the wind.

The screams ended, but the din went on throughout that day and well into the night: they had found the stores of wine and ale. I slept fitfully and woke early, cramped and cold, hungry and thirsty. From my concealment I saw them go at last, westwards again, singing in time to the stamp of their feet. It had rained in the night, and the sun was watery through ragged cloud. I let it rise a good hour longer before venturing down.

The scene was as I had expected: a tattered ruin of goods and men. I made my way through it to the Lady chapel. The chest which had held the abbey's treasure was smashed and empty. So was the smaller chest which had sheltered the holy dish. It had been wrenched from the wall and lay on the ground in splinters. The Abbot lay in front of it. Their axes had obliterated his face; I knew him only by his robe.

I followed the barbarians, though not closely and not in their immediate wake where all was devastated. A mile or so on either side of the swath of destruction, houses, even villages, had escaped unscathed, and out of thankfulness were generous to a vagabond. I slept that night in a comfortable bed. Next day, from a distance, I watched them storm the palace.

It did not take long, and by late afternoon they had moved on. They might have left a guard behind, to hold it as a strongpoint, and I knew I should wait and watch; but could not. Sword in hand – yet knowing how little use it would be against those murderous axes – I made my way through the shattered gate, stepping over the tree they had felled and lopped to batter it down.

Here what they had not smashed or plundered they had put to the torch: there was smoke in the air still and timbers smouldered underfoot; the roof of the great hall gaped to the heavens. Here, too, there were corpses I knew well.

And one who was not yet dead, though dying. My brother lay among a heap of bodies at the far end of the hall, where the last stand had been broken. His right leg was a bloody mess, and another blow had smashed one side of his face. But he opened the eye he still possessed. He spoke in a whisper, 'The little bear ...' His riven face twisted into what could either have been a smile or a grimace of agony. 'You must dance a better dance than I did, little bear.'

I said, 'I will,' and brought him water, and watched him till he died.

II

All that was long ago.

In the wake of the barbarian onslaught, survivors gathered. Among them was Flavius Rufus, and for ten years he ruled our war band before he fell in battle. I took over command, none challenging. I had a man's sword long before, and a man's horse.

We fought them ten years more, and twice ten years after that. At the beginning our attacks were scarcely more than gnat bites to a boar: we raided outlying camps and picked on bands of stragglers, relying on our horses to carry us quickly in and away. We skirmished only, knowing we were no match for them in the field. But as the years passed, our numbers increased and our power with it. We harried them ever more closely, and they first withdrew from their western outposts and after that, slowly and reluctantly, fell back towards the east.

It came to battles then, and victories. Twice they fled, to regroup and fight again. But in the third battle their backs were to the sea. Those that escaped were a beaten rabble, and thousands stayed to manure our fields. One such was their king. Nearby we found his hall, a wooden hut built large, and his treasure.

I did not look at it for two days: there were other things to do. The barbarians had left stores of ale too, and of the strong sweet liquor which sent them reckless into battle. I let my men loose on those, first appointing a few I could trust to guard the hall. When at last I went there they were at their posts, a little drunk but capable. I was proud of them: the rest of the army lay stupefied in sleep.

Someone else awaited me, a bishop named Oweyn. He was a true Celt in height and red hair, but thin and puny in appearance. He had been with us the past several months, and had offered Mass before the final battle.

He greeted me in the high speech but addressed me as 'Brenin', which is king in the native tongue. It was a custom which was growing, and I had grown tired of checking it. I asked him his business. He had come, he told me, to claim property which had belonged to the Church, before the savages stole it. Seeing my cold eye, he added that he was sure a ruler so mighty as I was lacked nothing in piety, either. Again, he called me Brenin.

I bade him follow me. The hall was as it had been left when they feasted before battle, the rough tables strewn with scraps of food, the rushes on the floor filthy and littered with drinking horns. The king's chamber was at the far end. It too was high-ceilinged, lit by a single window through which blew a breeze with the edge of autumn.

There were tapestries on the walls, of war and hunting scenes, several with gold wire woven through. Underfoot were skins, one from some great white beast. The royal bed was curtained and clothed in linen; its base was the chest which held the royal treasure. I pulled the mattress off, and lifted the lid. The chest was a good seven feet in length, not much less broad and high. It was more than three-quarters filled with articles in gold and silver, many ornamented with jewels.

I stood back from it, and the bishop, at my nod, began to rummage. With loving care he brought out dishes, ewers, candlesticks, a figure of the Christ bound to His cross. One thing I recognized: the monstrance that had hung before the altar in the abbey, when I was a boy.

I commanded his interest when I said so. He asked, like

a tremulous girl, if I had known Abbot Marcus. I told him yes.

'You are a fortunate man, sire, to have known the martyr – the saint who sacrificed his life in defence of the Holy Grail.'

'But did not save it.'

'He died for it. And from Heaven has guarded it, and now, through your hands, will restore it to the Church.'

I remembered the scene at the abbey, all those other bodies strewn over the stone flags. Some had met harder deaths, far harder. I asked, 'Do you think it is here?'

He scrabbled inside the chest, tossing costly ornaments aside in his eagerness. One was the gold torc which had been my father's. Then, with a sigh, he straightened up and turned to me again. He held a dish.

It was silver: less than two feet across, of no great substance, scratched and dented, tarnished almost black. I asked, scarcely able to believe, 'Is that your Grail?'

'Yes, Brenin. This is the dish from which our Lord and His disciples ate. The blessed martyr has preserved it.'

That, or plain accident. It surprised me that, having so much else more valuable, the barbarian had bothered to keep it with his treasure. He might easily have given it to his dog to drink from.

I said: 'Well then, all is restored.'

'This is.' He cradled the dish to his bosom. 'And I will guard it, God helping, with my life as he did.'

'And the rest.' I pointed to the gold. 'I have never seen such a store of wealth.'

He looked at the other things indifferently. 'They are nothing; but they will be of service in the rebuilding of our churches. There is ruin everywhere.'

What he said was true. We had won back our land but the

years of fighting for it had left a wasteland. It was not only churches that needed rebuilding.

And to what end? We had destroyed the power of the barbarians, and those that remained must do our will. For a generation, maybe two, we might hold that governance. But in time they would rebel, and others of their race would come from across the sea; and would there then be any with a will to resist them? I thought of my satisfaction with a guard that was not too drunk to fall asleep. The ancient virtues were lost, and would not be regained.

I turned the golden torc in my hands. The empire survived in the east, but we had no contact with it: other barbarians roamed unchecked across the places between. Of the City I knew only that it had been sacked many times since that first storming. If a Senate still existed it did so on the sufferance of its conquerors.

More than the land lay waste: customs and traditions also. The natives, to whom we had once given laws and culture, had resumed old ways: there were divisions everywhere and petty kings multiplied. It would not be an easy task to bring them together; but I must do it, even knowing that I preserved an empty shell, doomed to shatter before long.

I lifted the torc, but did not put it on. A gaudy ornament, my father had called it, and I would never wear the toga that might have dignified it. But yes, it would impress the natives, and those surviving barbarians I supposed we must call natives now. When I had accomplished what still remained to be done, I could wear it before the assembly of my subjects. They would hail me as High King, thinking it a nobler title than mere Governor.

They would think so, knowing no better.

That would be the bear's last dance. The tune I had learned as a boy had faded into silence. There were other tunes, and other dancers, but I was too old for the exercise.

Yet I could hold to the memory. And if the toga was denied me, I would manage without the bauble. I tossed the circlet of gold back into the chest. To the bishop, I said, 'Take that as well. Go and build your churches.'

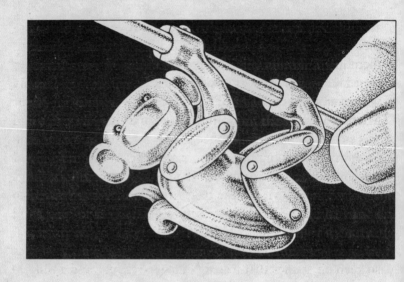

Monkey Business

GILLIAN AVERY

1938

'If you tell me why you want it,' Anne said, 'I might lend it.
Or I might not. It depends.'

'What does it depend on?' said the little sister. She didn't
care about it one way or another, but it was pouring with
rain; there was a long time until lunch and you had to fill in
the time somehow. She lay on the floor, concentrating on the
ceiling and trying to imagine what it would be like if you
were walking on it, like a fly.

'On why he wants it, of course.'

'I know why,' said Katie. She heaved her legs up until she
was balancing herself on her neck and shoulders.

'Why?'

'He's afraid of something at school, of course.'

They all went to boarding school – they had to because their parents lived in India and their aunt could only have them in the holidays. Anne was the sort of person who always coped capably with any situation; Katie settled happily wherever she was and didn't much care about anyone; it was Michael who worried and fretted and ran temperatures and was sick as the beginning of each new term approached. And for him it was going to be even worse this term as the school was moving, away from the familiar Surrey surroundings that he had known for the past two years, to somewhere in Wales where the headmaster had told everybody there would be 'room to expand'. Michael was sure he knew what that meant – more of those awful Scout games that Mr Beale was so keen on, games that tested your self-reliance and ability to keep your head.

Michael had his back turned so his sisters couldn't see his face. He was staring out at the drenched garden. School was at the back of his mind, but the black fog that oppressed him, hemmed him in, was because of the book he had rescued from the garden that morning. He had put it right at the back of the airing cupboard – at the bottom, under the hot-water tank. He had taken one or two looks at it since, but it was still sodden, though now stuck all over with bits of grey fluff.

'Is it that?' said Anne. 'Well, you might say something.'

'He's sulking,' said Katie. 'Nobody else in our family sulks,' she added self-righteously. 'If I could get a weeny bit higher I'd be standing on my head. Am I standing on my head now?'

'No, you aren't. Look, Michael, you can't get things out of people if you just mooch and stare out of the windows. You've got to ask properly.' She took her position as head of the family in their parents' absence very seriously. Even greater than the task of not letting Katie get above herself was the task of making a man of Michael. He flopped like jelly when life became difficult. He always seemed to be in trouble, not so much because of anything he did but because of things that happened to him. 'Michael lacks moral fibre,' Mr Beale had said in his last headmaster's report. It was what Anne had always thought. She had written to their parents to ask for advice but had had no reply yet.

'I did ask,' Michael said, watching two drops that ran down the pane. He wanted it more than he had ever wanted anything in his life. It was the only possible thing that could avert disaster. But even if the disaster about *The Boy's King Arthur* became known (and whatever he did to cover up disasters they seemed doomed to disclose themselves), he would be mute about the only thing he felt could rescue him: Anne's monkey on a stick charm, the mascot that she always took in her pencil box to exams. Nothing was going to drag out of him why he wanted it. As long as he wasn't told that it wouldn't work it might work.

There had been something left to hope for in all this misery. When he had woken up in the middle of the night and had heard the rain thundering down, hammering on the roof of the bay window below his bedroom, he had instinctively cast his mind to what he might have left out in the garden. Cricket bat? Tennis racket? His blazer? Then he remembered – the book that Mr Beale had put into his hands at the end of last term as a holiday task.

Large and expensive with a lot of coloured plates, it usually had to be read in the classroom under the supervision of a master (who also saw that your hands were clean). But Mr Beale had pressed it on him with the smile that made the school call him Sunny Jim (it was a smile that always froze Michael) – saying that it was to be a double task. It was not just to read: it was to test his powers of guardianship (which

58

Michael had just been lectured about, having in one week lost one cricket pad, one Latin grammar, two library books, the protractor which Greenaway had lent him and the Sherlock Holmes which was Mr Littlejohn's – it was later found with its cover badly mangled behind a shoe rack in the cloakroom). Mr Beale said he trusted Michael to bring it back in as good order as it had left the school. The library books were in fact being distributed among the boys for the holidays because of the school's impending move, but Michael knew that he had been allotted the pearl of the collection (given by Campbell ma. a year ago as a leaving present). And he knew why, and he knew that everybody else knew too. Not because he was good at looking after things, certainly not because of that.

He had found *The Boy's King Arthur* less than enchanting. He knew it was going to bore him from the cover picture of a knight on a horse sloshing another knight, and a fairy-tale sort of castle on a rock behind. It wasn't going to be about anything real; it was going to be Literature. However, he had dutifully opened it from time to time (even remembering to wash his hands first), though he had never got much further than 'It befell in the days of the noble Utherpendragon ...' Random investigation on other pages was not encouraging, and there were 320 of those. Of course he should never have taken it out into the garden, but he thought he might get on with it better there, away from Anne who was practising her Grade III piano pieces, and Katie who was stringing beads and dropping them all over the place, expecting him to help her find them. Then it was teatime and after that Utherpendragon and Sir Ector and the rest had disappeared from his mind.

And now the book was a pulpy mess lying under the tank with all the pages stuck together. Even if it got dry it could never look the same. Each time he had groped for it and pulled it out he had hoped it would not be as bad as he remembered. Invariably it was worse.

'He's probably worrying about his school being in a new place,' said Katie. 'About having to go to Wales.'

'Is it that, Michael?' said Anne with a professional, caring sort of voice.

'I suppose so.' It certainly was partly true. Surely it wasn't a lie if you didn't tell the whole reason? The monkey on a stick wouldn't work if you told a lie to get it, he was sure of that.

'But it's just the same people, Michael.'

That was precisely what the trouble was. He had always found with Anne that she made things worse when she was briskly trying to be comforting.

'Just in a different place,' she assured him. 'And nobody else will have seen it either.'

'Except Mr Beale,' said Katie in a muffled way. She was trying to do a back somersault and the skirt of her dress was over her face. 'He must have seen it,' she said, surfacing, 'he chose it.'

However, when Chart School reassembled, on platform one of Paddington station on September 27 1938, Michael did have, carefully wrapped in tissue paper and in its own box which he carried in his raincoat pocket, the monkey charm. It was very generous of Anne, who had her Grade III exam in November. Packed in brown paper, in the trunk that had been dispatched ahead of him, was the wreck of *The Boy's King Arthur*, dry now, but its cover curled and buckled. He had not dared try to open its pages, but he suspected it could not be done.

He had wrapped it up himself; nobody in the house yet knew about the catastrophe. Perhaps they need never know, if the mascot worked. When everybody else in church had been praying for peace – 'that the war clouds gathering over Europe may be dispelled' the vicar intoned, Sunday after Sunday – he had been praying that something would happen to Mr Beale. He knew what he would really like was for him to drop down dead, but also knew that you couldn't possibly pray for that, or even have it in your mind. So, squeezing his nails into his hands, pressing his knuckles into his eyes (to show how much he meant it), he asked that 'everything should be all right about the book' – meaning that either Mr Beale should come back to school blind so that he couldn't see its state, or else that he should have lost his memory so that he wouldn't ask for it, or, best of all (though he didn't like to suggest it), that he should be in hospital. Not with anything too painful, just a broken leg or something.

The book did have the effect of driving out worries about the new school. And it totally drove out any thought of war. All the talk about Hitler and Czechoslovakia, about schools being evacuated, the air-raid shelters that were being dug in Hyde Park (they had all seen them when Aunt Muriel had taken them up to London in early September to buy their school uniforms), he might take these in with his eyes but not with his mind. From the train that day they had also seen a barrage balloon, fat and silvery, floating in the distance. Anne knew all about them and what they were supposed to do, of course, and explained it to Katie who immediately produced all manner of reasons why balloons could not. But Michael had just stared dumbly out of the window into the sky and thought again about how Mr Beale was going to react when he heard about the book.

It would probably happen in front of other boys. Everybody in the class would be asked in turn for a report on holiday reading, eleven people would hand back clean, tidy books and Michael would have that lump of papier mâché, would stutter out what had happened, and Mr Beale would have that smile on his face and say terrible sarcastic things while the other boys turned round to see how Michael was taking it. Could he stop himself from crying? He did cry when things went wrong. To the amazement of masters and the contempt of other boys, and to his own fury, tears streamed out of him, reducing him to a blubbering, sniffing and gulping mess.

So when Aunt Muriel led him out of the underground at Paddington towards the crowd of boys in their navy blue raincoats and blue and white circled caps, he was not, as was usual, thinking despairingly about how he was going to say goodbye to Aunt Muriel (whom he didn't like all that much anyway) without his eyes flooding and spilling over. His thoughts had long passed beyond that, to the confrontation with Mr Beale.

It was a great relief to Aunt Muriel to see him dry-eyed. She went back home to Reigate and wrote to her brother and sister-in-law in India that Michael really did seem to be growing up at last and had gone back to school so bravely. And she went on to say what a good thing it was that his school was moving so far from London with all this dreadful talk of war and air raids and gas attacks. Especially as Mr Beale was such a reliable and understanding man.

Michael might have seemed brave to Aunt Muriel, but even she could not have described him as cheerful. He had dragged his way down the platform to the coach reserved for their school party and had settled in his seat with a face set in such blank misery that Mr Brewster, one of the masters who was escorting the boys, had asked him if he was feeling all right. (The other master, Mr Littlejohn, knowing Michael better, would not have asked such a dangerous question.)

Michael had to be prodded hard by a neighbour before he could even take in the question, and then just nodded dumbly.

As the train sped out of the grimy London suburbs into open country the other boys in the carriage questioned Mr Brewster, not about the war and what Mr Chamberlain was saying to Hitler, but about the new school. What was it like? Was it bigger than Chart in Surrey? Would there be other schools for them to play matches against? If it was so far from anywhere, would they get out of going to church? And how were they going to get to it from the station? Was it by taxi? Was Mr Beale there already? Had it gas-proof rooms? Hislop mi. asked, because his cousin's school had.

Mr Brewster said that Titleigh was only a tiny station, deep in the country, so there wouldn't be taxis, but it had been arranged that a bus should meet the train. No, he hadn't seen the school. Nobody had, except Mr Beale, and probably (Mr Brewster couldn't of course say for certain) he had been there all holidays making preparations and finding new staff. Hislop mi. wondered hopefully if perhaps there wouldn't have been time to find a music teacher. Merton started cataloguing aloud the things that would have had to be packed – the inkwells, the shoe racks, the school photographs – and everybody started thinking of more items, some of them ribald. And as Mr Brewster seemed for once to be turning a deaf ear, people got more and more daring.

With everybody engrossed in adding things like lavatory paper and chamber pots to the paraphernalia that would have to go in the furniture vans, Michael groped for the box in his pocket and unwound the mascot from its protective coverings. It was so small, less than an inch long: a monkey with jointed limbs that could be pushed up and down its

63

slender silver stick. Nobody knew where it came from, but it was never disputed that it was Anne's, and they all knew what good luck it had brought her – never less than 70 per cent in all her exams, and a Merit in Grade II piano when she had fallen off the gym ribstalls only the day before. And it had stopped her getting measles when he and Katie had had it last Christmas. It was quite powerful enough to help him; the only trouble was would it mind that it was him not Anne? And would it be offended by his doubting?

Oxford slipped by, its towers and spires glimpsed behind a huge gasometer. The train, slower now, chuntered through Cotswold villages. The other boys, who had exhausted the possibilities of removal vans and their contents, started looking at the comics that parents had bought for them at Paddington. By the time Malvern was reached they had finished these (even the swapping possibilities) and were beginning to think about tea. Malvern station had school trunks standing on it (you could recognize those anywhere) and a party of girls wearing purple school blazers; school and the ordeal ahead knocked at Michael's mind with renewed force. The sight of school buildings – chapel, playing fields – sprawling up the hills beyond the station made him feel sick and in no mood to add his voice to those who were planning their ideal tea.

Mr Brewster knew the route and could tell them when they reached Colwall that there was only one station before they got to Hereford, where they had to change. Only one. Michael wished there were a hundred; he wished they could go on chuffing through the countryside for ever. He wouldn't care about tea so long as he never had to see Mr Beale. He clutched at the box in his pocket, and he knew by the feeling in his throat that the tears were rising.

Hereford station and the scramble to the other train did

have the effect of suppressing them. Mr Brewster and Mr Littlejohn were running up and down counting boys, checking that everybody had the case with his pyjamas, toothbrush and house-slippers, and his cap on his head. Then they marched up the steps, over the bridge, down the other side and into another train which looked so old that Merton reckoned it was Victorian. But Merton was the only person who had the spirits to notice. Everybody else was tired, hungry and silent. Nobody seemed to expect any end to the journey, so that when after half an hour Mr Brewster called urgently 'Titleigh station, here we are,' and Mr Littlejohn came running down the platform banging at the windows, it was a surprise.

There were forty-one boys standing there in the grey, overcast late afternoon. Mr Littlejohn had counted them twice and that was right. And they all had their attaché cases and their caps and their blue raincoats. Watching the tiny speck of train disappearing (you could really only now see the plume of smoke), Michael plunged his hand into his pocket as he had done at five-minute intervals throughout the journey, to clutch the monkey in its box. But this time there was nothing there, nor in the other pocket. He pulled them inside out, he undid his raincoat and felt in every pocket of his grey flannel suit, though he knew it hadn't been put there. He pushed past the boys and peered down at the rails in case it might be lying there among the stones. Of course it was not. But then how could it not be in his pocket? He had pulled it half out and looked only seconds before Mr Brewster had told them that this was their station. On despairing, trembling legs he walked up the platform to where he thought they had got out, pausing all the time to scan the track and then the platform for a little white box. He walked right up to the end where the platform began to slope down and, with nowhere else to look, stood limply, hopelessly, staring into the distance.

When at last he turned round he found he was alone. Forty boys seemed to have vanished into thin air. They'd all gone, leaving him alone at the station! Then he saw they hadn't gone. The platform was very long (amazingly long for a place that didn't seem to be anywhere, that stood engulfed in trees), and everybody was standing in a huddle at the far end.

Nobody looked round when at last he reached them. Nobody said, 'Where on earth have you been?' or, 'Jackson, one day you'll be late for your own funeral.' They were staring at Mr Brewster and Mr Littlejohn and somebody who seemed to be the station-master, who certainly was very cross.

'And if them trunks aren't removed within twenty-four hours,' said the station-master, a fierce-looking man with bristling white whiskers, 'they're going to be pitchforked out of the parcels office, I'm telling you straight. And there's boxes into the bargain. And bikes cluttering up the place. Folks that move themselves into the country ought to see there's a place for them to go to before they leave where they've come from.'

There was a silence. Then one of the smallest boys, two forms below Michael, wailed, 'But how are we going to get to the school, if there isn't a bus, or taxis, or anything? Can't we tell Mr Beale?'

'That is just the trouble,' said Mr Littlejohn. 'Mr Beale isn't there. In fact, there doesn't seem to be a school at all.'

1987

'It was an extraordinary thing,' said Michael Jackson. 'Mr Beale, who was regarded so highly by all the parents, who

66

was supposed to have such a wholesome influence on us boys, had apparently pocketed the term's fees (paid in advance, of course) and made off. I heard much, much later, that he had also taken one of the boys' mothers. From what I could gather it was a sudden impulse. He had genuinely at the end of the summer term expected to move the school to that spot on the Welsh borders, but other things (notably Pringle's mother) had intervened, and he had never got there. Probably the house the school was supposedly moving into wasn't even his by the time the railway was trying to deliver all those trunks and tuck boxes and bikes.

'How on earth those two poor masters got us all home from the middle of nowhere I can't now remember, because I was knocked absolutely dizzy by the miracle that had happened. I had prayed that something might overtake Mr Beale and the monkey mascot had not only removed Mr Beale but the whole school! The other boys might chatter about what could have happened, but I knew that I, me alone, was responsible. I was trembling, I can tell you. And I was very glad that the monkey charm *had* disappeared. Even though it was going to be painful to tell my sister, it was obviously far too dangerous a thing to have in one's possession.

'Two things strike me now. One is how much children suffer from small disasters that adults would just brush aside (from that point of view it's a great relief to grow up).

'And the other is the irony of Mr Beale lecturing me about responsibility. I had mislaid books and cricket pads; he had mislaid forty-one boys.'

NOTE: The headmaster who dispatched boys to a non-existent school is a fact. I am grateful to Sir Malcolm Pasley, to whom this happened when he was a boy, for telling me the story.

Argos

RICHARD ADAMS

Hallo, cat: come to lie on the dungheap with me, have
you? Oh, ratting, eh? Well, there's plenty round here. Nowadays the whole place is full of rats – human ones, too. Might
have caught 'em myself once; not any more, not now.

All right, if you're going to watch that hole I can keep as
still as you. Keeping still – that's about all I'm good for now.
I'm run down: but no more than the whole place is run
down. Full of rats: and I'm full of fleas. Better mind you
don't catch a few.

How old are you, cat? A year? Two years? Too young to
remember much, anyway. Too young to remember the
better days. I suppose you won't believe I'm more than
twenty, eh? What's that you said? Don't hear well now, you
know. 'What's "twenty"?' did you say? Well, it's a lot of

68

years – very old for a dog. Very old indeed. I was a damned good dog once, though no one'd think so now. Not to look at me.

There's not an animal on the place now that remembers the master: only me. And even I wasn't much more than a puppy when he had to go away to the war. He'd begun training me, though. He told Diokles, the kennel-man, that he reckoned I was going to turn out such a fine hound that he'd train me himself. And so he did. I enjoyed every minute of it. We'd had some great times already and I was shaping up well. I could come when I was called, and wait where I was told and walk to heel – yes, through a herd of goats, if you like. I could follow scent, too: oh, couldn't I just? Everyone said I surely had the best nose in the world. The master used to say, give the two of us a year together and he'd take me anywhere: wolves, wild boar – the lot.

The way things turned out, though, it was precious little joy the master ever had of my marvellous nose. One summer morning – oh, that morning, I remember it as if it were yesterday! – we were just getting ready to go hunting, he and I. There was another, older hound with us, a dog called Kassos. Kassos – he's been dead for years now – I learned a lot from him. Diokles had just slipped our leads when suddenly the master stopped dead-still, looking down towards the harbour below us and the sea out beyond. There was a ship – not one of ours – still a goodish way out, but it was coming in towards the harbour all right. The master stood staring at it.

'I knew it!' he said at last to Diokles. 'I knew it! It's them! And we know what *they*'ve come for, don't we?'

He began walking backwards and forwards across the grass, biting on his fingers. 'I'm no coward,' he said. 'It's the oracle's prophecy that frightens me. The oracle said that if I went I wouldn't come back for years and years, and then it

69

would be alone and destitute. Yes, it's them all right: see the lion on the sail?'

'I'm afraid so, sir,' says Diokles. 'We'd all heard tell of the war, of course, but I'd been hoping they might leave us out of it. After all, it's not as though the island's all that big or full of men – not compared to that lot over at Mycenae.'

'They're scraping the barrel,' answers the master. 'That's what it is, Diokles: scraping the barrel. But they won't scrape me! Hurry, now! Go and get a plough and an ox and an ass, and bring them down to the beach: round the point, there, see? in the cove. I'll be down directly to tell you what to do.' He stooped down and patted me. 'I'm not called "the angry one" for nothing,' he says. 'I'm angry now all right, but I'm not such a fool as to let them see it.'

And with that he set off back to the house. He seemed to have forgotten about me, so I just trotted along behind him, waiting for orders. He went straight into the hall. The mistress was there, with the baby on her arm. She was talking to Eurycleia, but when she saw the look on the master's face she broke off and stared at him, sort of frightened.

'It's them, my love,' he said, jerking his thumb over his shoulder. 'I told you they'd be coming for me. But you do as I say, now, and we'll fool them yet. Give me that big salt-box by the fire, there. And remember, I've gone stark, raving mad. Tell all the servants – tell everyone. And mind you act up to it yourself. Cry your eyes out! Everything depends on convincing them.'

So then he kissed her and went out. Just at the door he met Eumaeus – that's the swineherd, you know, a decent fellow: he's almost the only one left that's still kind to me – coming in for orders. He didn't get any orders, though. The master just turned towards him, grabbed his cap off his head – a greasy old felt thing, it was, shaped like half an egg – and left him staring as the two of us headed for the shore.

When we got down to the beach, sure enough Diokles was waiting with the plough and the beasts.

'Yoke 'em up,' says the master, 'and then mind you stand back, because I'm not safe, understand?'

Then he started carrying on fit to terrify every man, bird and beast for miles. It even frightened me! He was frothing at the mouth and his eyes were rolling and staring – he didn't even blink, or not that I could see. Gods! he even *smelt* different, or that's how it seemed to me at the time, watching him.

'Harroo!' he said. 'Harroo! Sow the snow! Sow the snow!' And he began throwing salt over his shoulder as he went, and the two poor beasts lurching along in front of him looking just about as crazy as he did.

Then I saw the strangers coming. There were three of them, all dressed in armour, with purple plumes on their helmets and soldiers behind them to carry their shields and weapons. You could see they were important men – kings, I reckon they must have been. The mistress was with them, still carrying the baby on her arm. She was crying her eyes out, just like the master had told her.

'He's been like this for five days,' she was sobbing to the kings as they came up to us. 'Five days! It's the madness of the goddess! He's cursed – cursed! He'll die, I know he will! O Zeus, take pity on us! Take pity on a poor woman!' And she began tearing her hair.

Eumaeus was just behind her. 'He's not safe, my lord,' he says to the king next to him. 'He killed the stableman yesterday: struck him down with an oar and said he was threshing the corn. Now you've seen for yourself, my lord, I'd come away before someone gets hurt. He doesn't even know his wife from his hound.'

Then the mistress gave the baby over to Eumaeus and went and stood right in the master's way. She held up her arms and called out to him, but he simply drove the beasts straight at her and threw salt all over her hair and her robe, and she only just jumped clear in time. She flung herself into the arms of one of the kings, screaming.

'He'd have ploughed over me!' she cried. 'His own wife! Oh, was there ever a house so afflicted! Pray, good sirs, only take pity on us and leave us to try and calm him! Strangers only make him worse!'

'What do you reckon, Palamedes?' says one of the kings. 'I'm afraid we've had our journey for nothing. Poor fellow, he seems very bad.'

'Just a moment,' says the man called Palamedes. He went across to the mistress, who'd just taken the baby back from Eumaeus, and snatched him out of her arms. The master wasn't looking: he was just turning the beasts round to plough another stretch of the sand.

Palamedes laid the baby down straight in his way. 'Let's see whether he knows *him*,' he said, and he held the mistress back with his two hands on her shoulders. 'If he ploughs on now, I'll believe it.'

The master came straight on, still shouting and yelling, and for a moment I thought he was going to plough the baby. But then he slowed down. He faltered and stopped. You could see he meant to: you could see he knew what he was doing. The baby was crying – all the noise and the big men had frightened him. The master went forward, picked him up in his arms and began soothing him.

'Not quite good enough, eh?' says Palamedes, going up to him quite friendly and putting a hand on his shoulder. 'Can't say I altogether blame you, though. If you like I'll give you a hand getting your weapons and armour together.'

72

Well, at that Diokles took hold of my collar, turned on his heel and led me away up the cliff. He put me back into the kennels, so I didn't see the master preparing to go away to the war with the kings. Kassos did, though: he was under the table in the hall when the master ate his last dinner and drank his last bowl of wine.

It was getting on for sunset when the master came round to the kennels himself. I heard him calling to Diokles.

'I want Argos!' he said. 'Bring him out here.'

They were all there in the yard – the mistress, the kings, everyone. The master had the baby in his arms. He went down on one knee beside me and held the baby up against my nose. I remember the smell of new flesh and women's milk: I remember it now.

'Argos,' says the master, 'I'm going away – for a long time, most likely. This is Telemachus. You're to guard him, do you understand? Night and day. You're never to let him out of your sight until he grows to be a man. You're to run with him and hunt with him and sleep beside him. You're to guard him; and you're to guard your mistress, too, because I shan't be able to.'

He was crying. His tears were falling all over my muzzle.

'One day I shall come back, Argos,' he said. 'Don't you ever forget it! One day I'll come back and require it of you – this guardianship of yours. You always were the best dog of the lot, and you shall have your reward. The grey-eyed goddess will look after me; and she's the one who'll give you your reward, too.'

So then he went away on his ship and I never saw him again. No one has, from that day to this. All my life the island's been left without a king – left to go to pieces. Well, who could take *his* place? That old man Mentor: I know he's

73

always done his best, but he's never been much good, really. I guarded Telemachus, though, no danger. He grew up, and I grew up with him. I went with him when he began toddling along the shore, and I went with him when he got old enough to go out and play with the other children. Oh, they all learnt to know me. There was a hefty boy – Eumastus, he was called – who used to wait until there weren't any grown-up people about and then shout 'Where's your fa-ther?' One day Telemachus turned and went for him, and Eumastas knocked him down: he was so much bigger, you see. But after I'd finished with him he was limping for a month. He never said it again.

When Telemachus got old enough to go hunting with Diokles, he always used to take me with him as his personal hound. Diokles had finished my training, of course, and I can tell you, cat, there wasn't a hound in the whole kennels could keep up with me. 'Podas Argos' they used to call me: the Flashing-footed! I was like a thunderbolt in those days. There wasn't a wild beast could get away from me, even in the thickest woods, and I was the best hound on a scent in all the island. Everyone knew it.

All the time, of course, I was waiting for the master to come back: but he never did. Some said he was dead. I couldn't believe it. After all, he himself had said plain enough that he was coming back; and he'd said the goddess would reward me, so I went on believing him. But now – now I don't know what to think.

I remember, one cold winter's night in the kennels, Kassos called me over to him. He was very old by that time: white-muzzled, and getting on for blind.

'Have you heard the news?' he said. 'That war thing – whatever it was – it's over, or so they're all saying.'

'Who won?' I asked.

'Our lot won, apparently,' he said. 'So now I suppose the master'll be coming home.'

Kassos died soon after that. But still the master didn't come back: and still I went on guarding Telemachus. He was eleven or twelve by that time – coming up for a youth. Often, in the evenings, he used to take me with him to the cliff-top, and we'd sit looking out over the dark sea.

'He *will* come back, Argos,' he'd say. 'The goddess has spoken in my heart and told me so. He will come back – just when we least expect it, I dare say.'

But it was the suitors who started arriving, not the master. Well, that's what they called themselves – suitors. First just four or five, and then more and more of them. They gave out that the master was dead and the mistress had got to choose one of them for a new husband. But that was all just a lot of pretence and lies. They'd come to eat up our food, kill our beasts and live off our land, that's what. Yes, and they even helped themselves to the girls, too. That nasty little tart Melantho – I never did like her: bone-lazy and dirty with it – she fairly loved every minute. She's inside with one of them now, damn her.

Telemachus tried to send them packing. But what could *he* do, just a bit of a lad against all those bullies? When they weren't insulting him, they simply ignored him. And all the time they kept on telling the mistress she had to choose. She used to take me with her to her room at night, for fear one of them would break down the door and force her. A lot of the day she used to spend weaving at her loom; but then, when we were alone at night, she'd unpick it all again. I never did understand why.

Things went from bad to worse, and at last I got too old to be any more good. Couldn't run; couldn't hear properly; teeth going, too. Diokles was dead, and the new kennel-man

75

didn't like me: he wanted younger dogs. All the same, I was all right as long as Telemachus was still around. *He* wouldn't stand by and see me ill-treated. He kept me with him even though I could hardly follow him about any more. That was one of the things the suitors used to jeer at him for. 'You and your mangy old dog!' It was that bastard Antinous said that, and they all laughed. And then another one – Agelaus, it was – said he supposed by this time the master must look just like me, if he was still alive. Have you any idea, cat, what it's like to be despised and insulted by men you could once have chased over the cliff?

Ah, but that's not the worst of it either, not by a long way. What's broken my heart happened about a month ago. Telemachus went away – yes, secretly, in a ship. And he wouldn't take me with him. It's the only time we've been apart in all the years since the master left.

One evening it was, just about this time of day. He'd been talking to old Eurycleia – her as used to be his nurse when he was a baby. They were up in the treasure-chamber. He'd left me outside, in the shade, while he went in to talk to her. When he came out he went across to the hall, where all the suitors were busy stuffing our grub and swilling our wine. It wasn't long before they were all as drunk as maenads, and soon after that they weren't even making a row any more: they'd either gone to sleep in the hall, or else staggered off to – well, to other beds. Telemachus bent down and patted me.

'Argos,' he said – just like the master, long ago – 'Argos, I'm going away. The ship's waiting for me now. I'd like to take you, Argos, believe me I would, but at your age you'd never stand the journey. But I'm coming back, d'you understand? I'm coming back *soon*.'

I've heard that tale before, I thought; and I can tell you my heart fairly sank into the ground. He was all I had left, you see. If he went, there'd be no one at all to care a curse what happened to me. I felt so desperate that I even tried to follow him, but he went off very quickly – him and old Mentor together. At least, I thought it was old Mentor: only I couldn't be sure. It looked like old Mentor, but somehow it didn't smell like him. And the funny thing was, next day Telemachus was gone right enough, but Mentor was still about.

It was after that that the really bad time began. I've just been left to die by myself, that's what it comes to. I'm forced to hang about the kitchen door for scraps – me, Podas Argos as used to be! – and I'm lucky if I get any, at that. I'm full of vermin; can't exercise; can't get as far as the stream, even. That blasted Antinous wanted to put a spear through me the other day, only old Eurycleia begged him not to. All the same, she's forgotten about me now, just like everybody else.

Hallo, who's this coming? Can't see anything against this sunset. Why, it's Eumaeus, the swineherd! Haven't seen him around for a day or two. He'll remember me, though, I'm sure he will. With any luck he might even give me something to eat. But – but who on earth's that with him? Why, it's an old beggar-man. He looks almost as thin and grey as I am! Whatever's *he* doing, limping along on a stick beside Eumaeus? And why's Eumaeus bringing him up here, for Zeus' sake? Now that's a thing I'll be damned if I'm going to put up with – beggars round the house! I may be old and done for, but I can still see a beggar off. Out of the way, cat, while I get on my feet.

Now, then, you! On your way! Oh! What – what is it? What's happened? That smell, that smell – it can't be! It – it's the master! It's the master! He's come back! And there's someone standing behind them! It's the goddess – it's the grey-eyed goddess! She's smiling – she's beckoning to me!

77

Gods, what a fool I am! I've been asleep. I've been dreaming! I dreamt – why, I dreamt the master had gone away, and the house was full of villains, and Zeus knows what else besides! And it was all just a stupid dream! Just a dream! I'm young! I'm strong! Podas Argos, that's me! We're going hunting, and the goddess – the goddess is coming with us! O master, dear master, here I am! Here I –

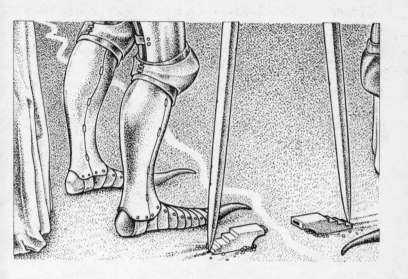

The Keeping of the Castle

BARBARA WILLARD

'NEVER!' shouted Sir Reginald.

'Be damned to you!' roared Sir Walter.

Godfrey, who was there at the meeting because he was acting as his father's page, glanced at Oswald, the steward, and Oswald rolled his eye – he had lost the other in battle years ago – and scratched at his little grey beard. He jerked his head towards the wine jug. Godfrey seized it and went swiftly, if nervously, to refill the two empty goblets. They were very beautiful silver goblets studded round the base with precious stones, some of which had fallen out and been lost – or more probably pocketed by whoever happened to be cleaning them at the time.

Godfrey stepped back quickly as Sir Walter rose, kicking

away the heavy oak stool with such force that it crashed on its side.

'Very well,' he almost snarled, 'there is nothing more to be said.'

'There never was anything to be said,' snapped Sir Reginald. He had some slight advantage since this was taking place in his castle, three or so miles across country from Sir Walter's.

Every inch of Sir Walter, a big man, bristled and almost sparked, as he strode for the door. The rushes on the floor stirred at his passing, and one rather withered fragment attached itself to his left spur. The huge door thudded behind him.

'The next time that tyrant rides this way,' Sir Reginald cried to his steward, 'see that the drawbridge is raised against him.'

Oswald bowed but said nothing, having known his master since he was a lad. Anyone might think that raising the drawbridge was no more of an effort than raising a finger.

Sir Reginald shoved his wine cup across to Godfrey.

'Fill it! Fill it to the brim!'

'Sir Walter was horribly angry, sir.'

'And so was I. Not only was he asking for your sister's hand in marriage with his son – but her dowry was to be the south side of the Fair Valley! Did you hear that?'

'Why should Sir Walter want the south side so very much, sir? He has the north side, after all, and the stream in the bottom that divides them is very clearly the boundary line between his lands and ours. Oswald has told me that and so has Brother Adrian. It all seems rather absurd.'

'It is absurd – though you are an impertinent monkey to say so. Still, I see you are being well taught. As my son and heir should be. As for Sir Walter, his great-grandmother's

80

uncle was second cousin to the king, and so he believes himself all-powerful. But my great-grandfather's third cousin
once removed was, if you remember, related to –'

'Excuse me, sir!' said Godfrey, who had heard all this too
often, 'I think I hear my mother calling . . .'

And without heeding his father's enraged cry to him to
'Stop!' he was across the hall and up the little winding stair
to his mother's quarters before Sir Reginald found breath for
a second bellow.

'Men are all the same,' his mother said. 'They never will
settle. They both know perfectly well that the stream in the
valley bottom is the natural boundary. But will they accept
it? No. Each craves the opposite bank. Your father could
have no possible use for the north bank. The south is a different matter. Why, it is so sweet and sheltered there it
would be quite perfect for a vineyard.' She turned back to
her spindle, where the yarn had become nastily knotted.
'Men are such ninnies, you know.'

Godfrey grinned. His mother, Lady Grizelda, was beautiful and wise, but best of all her virtues was her loving skill in
ridiculing her husband's frequent pomposities.

'Why was the matter discussed today?' she asked.

Godfrey glanced at his sister, who sat before her tapestry
frame looking bored. She was a couple of years his junior and
he, at this time, was fifteen.

'You'll never guess, madam – it's so amazing. Sir Walter
asked for our Isabella's hand in marriage with his only
son!'

Their mother laughed. 'You hear that, daughter? Ah –
that's woken you up, I see. Your first offer of marriage! No
wonder you are blushing. What was her dowry to be,
Godfrey?'

81

'What would you expect mother? The south side of the Fair Valley.'

'That means the offer was rejected.'

'It was rejected.'

'What a relief!' cried Isabella, though she looked the least bit put out.

Sir Reginald's castle was the old-fashioned sort, with a round keep. It perched on a convenient hill with an excellent view of the surrounding countryside. Just within sight, a little to the west, stood Sir Walter's castle. It had a square keep in the modern style, proving him little more than a newcomer. Between the two castles the land swooped down to that Fair Valley which meant so much to both, though for very different reasons. Sir Reginald wanted the whole valley for himself, while Sir Walter wanted the second part of it to please his French-born wife, Lady Madelena, cousin to the Duke of Burgundy.

Lady Madelena longed for what Lady Grizelda had seen might be possible – a vineyard planted on the south side of the valley. Lady Madelena was extremely vexed when Sir Walter returned with the news that the hoped-for deal had been rejected.

'I should have gone myself! Men are so clumsy and quick-tempered!'

The King, at this time, was mounting a Crusade to the Holy Land and he called on Sir Reginald to ride with the rest. There was nothing he could do about this. The King was his liege lord and had to be obeyed. He owned all the land, and to be called upon for the occasional armed adventure was the rent owed to him by tenants such as Sir Reginald.

'These travels often take years,' he said to Lady Grizelda. 'My dearest wife – you will forget my face.'

'No,' she said, smiling. 'But you will have opportunity to forget mine. Do not, I pray, return with some eastern-eyed damsel as your slave, as poor old Sir Basil did a few years ago.'

'My dear – please . . .' And he glanced at his young son and daughter as if fearing they might understand too much.

'You will have plenty to occupy you, husband – getting there and slaying infidels when you arrive – and gathering up treasure on the way, as so many others have done. But how shall we contrive till your return?'

'You will have the keeping of the castle. Godfrey, you are the only son I have, so you must be lord in my absence.'

'Yes, sir,' said Godfrey, more frightened than flattered.

'Ah well,' sighed Sir Reginald, 'I must set about it. Men . . . provisions . . . horses . . . The King absolves me from my knight-service hereafter – we must pay our dues peacefully from now on. And of course,' he said, pulling himself together with an obvious effort, 'a Crusade is a solemn business. The King honours me in sending me to further the cause of Christianity in the land of the heathen.'

Sir Walter's son was called Robert. Sir Walter spoke to him much as Sir Reginald had spoken to Godfrey – for he, too, had been called by the King to join the Crusade.

'I leave you, my boy, to take charge over all my lands. Guard the castle against intruders and see that your mother is well attended. And should I never return – for not every crusader returns to lie in peace in his own church – then I trust you to live honourably and carefully, but bravely.'

'Yes, father. Yes, sir,' said Robert, biting his lip, for he loved his father and the thought of losing him had filled his eyes with tears.

'A Crusade is a solemn business,' sighed Sir Walter, just as Sir Reginald had done. 'The King honours me in sending me to further the cause of Christianity in the land of the heathen.'

At first, after the departure of the lords and their followers, there was a hush that amounted to gloom. The young and lively men had all gone marching off, leaving behind their fathers, uncles and grandfathers. There was none of the usual bawling in the guardroom, where these older men were now on duty and quite content to sit down and play chess, or simply nod off. Isabella found her tapestry more boring than ever, Godfrey kept yawning at his lessons with Brother Adrian, and their mother sat a long time staring out of a turret window from which she could – almost – see the sea.

Everyone was thinking of the absent warriors; not only Godfrey, Isabella and Lady Grizelda, but Robert and his mother Lady Madelena, too.

The travellers had been gone three weeks or so when suddenly the wind changed, the air grew soft, the light brightened over all the land and it was spring.

Everyone immediately felt more lively.

'There must be lambs, brother,' said Isabella. 'Shall we go and look for them?'

These two were the best of friends. Isabella was bright and shrewd and the countryside brought out the best in her. She picked up her long skirts, tucked them into her waistband, pulled off her veil and used it to tie back her long fair hair. Brother and sister stamped together over the soft new turf, the larks rising before them.

'There!' cried Isabella. 'The lambs! And, oh, the daffodils! Oh – oh – *oh*! How beautiful everything is!'

'Do stop screeching – you sound quite mad. You've frightened the shepherd lad.'

But the boy who turned to them was rather too comfortably dressed for a shepherd lad, and seeing Isabella he took off his cap and bowed as no shepherd lad would know how.

The reason was simple. He was Sir Walter's only son, Robert.

As the weather grew ever softer, the countryside increasingly embroidered, Godfrey sought out Robert and Robert sought out Godfrey. After carefully sounding out one another's thoughts and opinions, they decided eventually on eternal friendship and brotherhood. They covered all the countryside round about both on foot and on horseback, and Isabella frequently joined them.

'I am in trouble with my tutor,' Godfrey told Robert one day, as they rode along the boundary stream and into the far woods. 'Brother Adrian complains that I am neglecting my lessons.'

'Brother Martin says the same to me, Godfrey. But Wilfred, my father's steward, who teaches me how I must manage my estates when I inherit, he says I'm learning the land, and he likes that.'

'It is the same with Oswald, Robert. He says I'm learning the land by leaps and bounds. We shall be the better overlords then, when our turn comes.'

They they were silent, for inheritance and lordship could not come while their fathers lived, and they were neither of them lacking in affection.

While these friendships were ripening, while the tutors grumbled and the stewards praised and Isabella recalled secretly that Robert's father had thought her a suitable bride for his son, the two mothers, lonely and dejected, a little warily sought one another's company. How good it would be, each thought, if in the absence of their lords, relations between castle and castle might be brought to sense and cordiality.

So on a warm day each rode out alone and by good fortune met at the stream that was the boundary between Sir Reginald's land and Sir Walter's land. Soon they were meeting regularly, delighting in intelligent company, for both suffered from a sad lot of sillies among their women. Thus they sat together reading, playing the lute and discussing such interests as distilling and preserving, the treatment of sickness with this herb or that – and gardening.

Lady Madelena took Lady Grizelda to her walled garden where once, indeed, she had grown herbs but where for many years now she had cultivated vines.

'The stock is from my own homeland, where my brother's vineyards are famous. We have a small distillery in a disused dungeon. You must taste the wine one day, dear madam. Indeed – why not today?'

Lady Grizelda rode home thoughtfully. The wine certainly was delicious. They had sipped it and discussed at length and had parted very cheerfully. But of course Lady Madelena was right in saying more space was needed ... some slope with a southern aspect?

Lady Grizelda sent for Godfrey.

'Never!' cried Godfrey, trying to sound like Sir Reginald. 'This is the very idea my father most detests.'

'No one mentioned a vineyard.'

'Impossible! My father will think me a traitor!' He deepened his voice, which sometimes defied him. 'Impossible, madam.'

'You are not yet the lord of this manor, my sharp young sir,' said his mother, not loudly but coldly. 'Keep the castle, by all means. But I will not be told what is best to be done by my own young son. The vineyard,' she concluded, turning her back on him, 'will be jointly owned. That is the end of the matter. Be off with you, child.'

Through that fine summer they prepared the ground, terracing up the steep south bank of the Fair Valley. Tiring work for the men left at home, and the two ladies were severe taskmasters. Wilfred's men worked better than those under Oswald's orders, who could not help wondering what Sir Reginald would do to them when he came home.

Then Lady Madelena's brother came from Burgundy with many vines for planting, and endless advice on their cultivation and eventual harvesting.

Time was passing at an extraordinary rate. A year, eighteen months – could it be so long since the departure of the two lords? In fact it was two years before any word came of Sir Reginald and Sir Walter. Then a messenger arrived in atrocious weather, bringing letters. Both gentlemen seemed in fairish health. Sir Reginald had had some slight fever and Sir Walter had broken his left little finger in an unfortunate fall from his horse. The heathen, it was clear, were so guileful and fought so fiercely that things went slowly. There was no word of a return.

By the following summer the vineyard began to look promising, and no one any longer made pretence of thinking it all a dangerous waste of time. There was more labour by now, as many boys who had been children when their fathers marched off, were old and strong enough to work. They were young men now – just as Godfrey and Robert had become young men and Isabella a decidedly beautiful maiden. And just about then, further letters arrived. They were short, their tone was subdued, the messenger was weary and unwilling to talk. Not yet, not yet . . . the letters seemed to say.

Godfrey and Robert had by now been keeping their fathers' lands for several years and had become practised in all that this meant – in ploughing and seeding and harvest, in provisioning for winter and the bringing in of fuel. One or two of the older people in each castle had died and been buried, and both Brother Adrian and Brother Martin had abandoned the pretence of teaching pupils who, in many ways, now knew more than they did. Of the boys who had become men, one was now appointed armourer and another had charge of the watch and of look-out duties.

So that when – at last and yet suddenly – news came that the warriors had returned, were disembarked and would soon set foot on their own soil, Godfrey and Robert experienced quite different emotions. For Robert there could only be a joyful reunion with his father, and the chance of getting married to Isabella; but for Godfrey there came a very strange pang of heart and conscience.

He feared greatly what his father might say when he saw the vineyard, which by now was flourishing – the distilling part of the business had spread to a second dungeon – and dreaded the accusation that he had betrayed his trust. Besides this, he had become accustomed to using his authority – it would be hard to give it all up with a smile. As for Robert and Isabella, Sir Reginald, if he raged, could put an end to their hopes.

It was decided to ride out and meet the returned wanderers and bring them home in triumph. A tidy company set out – the two wives, the two sons, the one daughter, each with suitable attendants. Oswald, his grey beard now quite white, ordered the company. Wilfred remained behind to make certain that on both castles the standards and banners were raised in welcome at precisely the right moment. Considerable tension held the cavalcade and all rode silently, the ladies close together for mutual encouragement, Robert and Isabella close together because they feared parting. Godfrey rode a little behind, Oswald at his elbow, clearly for support.

A little after noon, they saw in the bright September sunshine a very small party approaching, breasting a hill and moving slowly down the nearer slope. Sir Reginald and Sir Walter were riding side by side, attended by no more than three shabby servants between the two of them.

The welcoming party spurred forward, then halted. The two ladies were the first out of the saddle and running forward, arms outstretched. The sons, the daughter, hung back, unwilling to intrude.

Then Isabella cried out, almost wailing, 'They have changed! Oh – how they have changed!'

As all dismounted and mingled with cries of greeting, the fullness of the change was seen. A man stepped forward, holding out his hands to Godfrey – but was this truly his father? Sir Reginald's hair that had been dark and strong and curling was now white and thin, his beard was thin, his eyes weak and watery. His hands shook as he caught hold of his children, while behind stood Lady Grizelda, white-faced and weeping.

Sir Walter, too, had suffered, but being the younger man he had been better able to withstand the ordeals of the past years. His hair, too, was at least streaked with white, and he bore a long scar down all one side of his face that puckered his right eye and touched the corner of his mouth.

'Such change, my dear husband,' Lady Madelena murmured.

'Yes, yes, we are changed,' he agreed, putting his arm round her. 'But so, dear soul, are all here. The time has been long for all.'

Godfrey could not speak. He could think only of the change they had made in the Fair Valley, and how it lay between here and home.

They rode home slowly. From the last bend in the road it was possible to see both castles. There must have been shouts from the look-out, for instantly the banners shook out in the breeze and the two buildings were draped in a bright welcome. A far trumpet call was echoed by one nearer.

As they looked towards the castles they also looked directly down the Fair Valley, where the sun shone fervently on the vineyard.

Sir Reginald pulled in his horse. Sir Walter, too. The little cavalcade, curiously diminished by apprehension, straggled to a halt.

Isabella said softly, though her voice shook, 'It is beautiful, isn't it, sir? The vineyard is so beautiful!'

Sir Reginald did not reply. He sat there trembling, his hands clenched on the bridle, and Sir Walter watched him anxiously. The light, itself the colour of wine, poured over the valley and the vines showed strong and burgeoning. But still Sir Reginald chewed at his straggling moustache, and the conflict in his lined and colourless face stirred Godfrey almost to sickness.

'I must rest,' Sir Reginald said at last, muttering it through his clenched teeth. 'Take me indoors with you, friend.'

'Yes, yes!' cried Sir Walter. 'I shall be your host. And we shall learn together of what has been so well done in our absence.'

For a second it seemed as though Sir Reginald might

summon up strength enough to strike him – but the moment passed.

Only Godfrey rode home, Oswald still in support. Sir Reginald having decided to remain that night under Sir Walter's roof, his wife and his daughter stayed with him. As the two wives followed their husbands, they had exchanged a tremulous but hopeful smile, while Robert and Isabella had clasped hands in quick encouragement.

It was long after noon the next day when Sir Reginald returned and sent for Godfrey.

He was sitting back in his great chair, with his hands on the arms and his eyes closed as if too exhausted to begin speaking. Then his eyes slowly opened and for all their red rims they still held the shrewdness and the sharpness of a man who knew how not to appear beaten.

'I humbly beg your forgiveness, father,' Godfrey said, thinking it best to get in the first word.

Sir Reginald frowned. 'For what? Oswald here tells me you have kept the castle and all about it as well as any could. Even as well as I could.'

'But the valley, sir! The south side of the Fair Valley . . .'

'Well? Yes? What of that? As your sister said, very beautiful. An enterprise ordered by the ladies, I am told.' Now his voice was strengthening and he sat up straighter. 'Naturally there will be much to discuss. War makes enemies of friends, my son, but strangely it makes friends of enemies. Sir Walter and I have relied on one another. We are now brothers.'

'I am glad, sir. And so will my mother be and Lady Madelena. And my sister. And Robert.'

'We must be practical. Lawyers. We need lawyers.'

'Of course! For the marriage contract! For Robert and Isabella.'

'Yes, yes, that too, that too,' his father said, impatiently. 'But I am thinking of the vineyard. Sir Walter and I have lost all we ever had and gained only a very little glory in exchange. The vineyard will be our salvation. Dues to the King – vats of fine wine – what better?' He rose and began a tottering pace about the room. 'You will have to continue your labours, I fear, Godfrey. The manor is so large and demanding. I shall keep my energies for business matters. You will have to put up with it, you know.'

'Of course,' agreed Godfrey, not knowing whether to laugh or cry, not daring to glance in Oswald's direction.

'We must not forget,' his father said sternly, 'that although the vineyard stock is Sir Walter's, the land remains mine. The south side of the Fair Valley is mine and always will be.'

One day, Godfrey thought, it can only be mine, and Robert and I will be brothers and there will be no quarrel . . .

'Of course, sir,' he said out loud, nodding yet again in agreement.

'Send for Brother Adrian. I dare say he has sense enough to draw me some sort of deed . . . Where's Oswald?'

'I am here, my lord.'

'Bring me some wine, Oswald. And let it be the young wine from the Fair Valley vineyard. We must see that our cellars are stocked with all we are entitled to. The south side of the valley, after all, is mine.'

Jinnie's Chance

WINIFRED CAWLEY

A LONG time ago, when grannies were young, there was a girl called Jinnie.

She could stand longer and walk farther on her hands than anybody else in Stratford Street. What was more, she was the only one who could do the crab. It made her friend Mary shudder to watch her stand on her hands, drop her legs backwards, then crawl upside down half the length of the street before collapsing in a heap.

She could skip longer. She could run faster. She could throw a ball higher *and* catch it. When they played hot rice or rounders, she could belt the ball farther. She could whistle louder than any lad. When there was a hoy-oot at a wedding at the church at the end of Stratford Street where she and Mary lived, she got most of the pennies. But nobody minded, because she bought sweets and shared them before handing the rest of the money to her Aunt Lizzie.

She was never scared. Not of Mary's Dad. Not of Alice Boyes' Dad who lived in the next street, and he was a policeman. Not of Father Kelly who came from time to time and managed to scare some of his erring flock to church for a mass or two. Not of her teachers, not even the bad-tempered ones. When Miss Johnson of Standard Five threw a board rubber at her, Jinnie threw it back. Yet Miss Johnson didn't haul her off to Miss Cheeseman, the Headmistress. She would have if it had been Mary or one of the others. After this, Jinnie's fame spread through the whole school and her classmates thought there was no one like her.

She was three years older than Mary and Mary's other friends. It was a wonder she bothered with them. But they were glad she did: being with Jinnie was an adventure. Sometimes she led a whole troop of them down under the railway bridge to Anderson's farm to mess about in the duckpond until the farmer came and chased them. Or to the Daisy Hill to pick daisies, may blossoms or wild roses, and in winter to sledge down on boxes or bits of cardboard. Or to the Park to watch the tennis and bowls and make remarks and be chased by the park-keepers. Or across the High Street to the posh houses on the Green to play knockie-door neighbour.

'If she has to get bairns into mischief,' Mary's Dad said, 'why doesn't she stick to her own age?'

Mary's Mam said Jinnie usually did. 'It's the young ones that pester *her*. And she never swears or talks dirty like some I know.' Mam and Dad weren't arguing, just saying opposite things. 'Anyway,' Mam said, 'Jinnie's tricks are only what any bairn might get up to, which says a lot for Jinnie, considering the way she's been dragged up. Poor little lass, just left to grow up any old how.' Mam sighed and shook her head. She often did about Jinnie.

But Mary wasn't sorry for Jinnie. She envied her and wouldn't have minded being like her. Not that she would have swopped places with her. It was only what Jinnie *was* that she envied. To begin with, she wouldn't have liked not having a dad. Jinnie's father had been killed in the Great War and her mother's pension wasn't enough to rent a place of their own. So Jinnie lived with her Grandad and her Aunt Lizzie, while her mother went away to service. On Tyneside in those days that was the only job which didn't pay women starvation wages. Her mother was a housekeeper, Jinnie boasted. 'A maid of all work, poor soul,' Mam said, 'or worse.' But Jinnie's mother wasn't a poor soul any more than Jinnie was. She had nicer clothes than other Stratford Street mothers and was better-looking.

Nor would Mary have liked living with Jinnie's Grandad. He had an allotment near the Park and it was for ever needing manure. Often, too often, Jinnie was seen dragging along a nasty great box on wheels and collecting horse-muck. Lots of horses still went along Stratford Street pulling milk floats and bakers' vans, dust carts, fish carts, Rington's tea van and the fever van. So Jinnie's barrow, and Jinnie too sometimes, were pretty smelly.

Mary would have liked living with Jinnie's Aunt Lizzie even less. The good hidings she gave Jinnie – nobody knew exactly why – were awful. Mrs Charlton, who lived in the flat above Aunt Lizzie, could hear everything. Mary's Mam and Mrs Charlton agreed it was a wonder poor Jinnie hadn't had all the stuffing knocked out of her long ago. As it was, Jinnie had plenty of stuffing left: enough to be the sworn enemy of Mary's Dad, and that needed real stuffing.

Stratford Street and Jinnie liked Mam but didn't care

much for Dad. Because of his shop, Mam said. It was a tick shop, where you could get things and not pay until the end of the week – but Dad wouldn't give tick to just anybody. Even the women who were allowed tick didn't always get everything they asked for, especially not cigarettes if Dad thought their bill was already big enough that week. Or, if they had a food ticket from the Guardians, he wouldn't allow luxuries like sweets or sardines and write them down as margarine or flour. There were sometimes nasty rows about this.

Mam tried to explain to Mary: 'Nobody likes people with tick shops. *You* wouldn't if the boot was on the other foot. Mind you, your Dad should never have been in a shop.' She shook her head. 'What he really should have been is a preacher. There's not a soul at chapel can touch him when it comes to talking, not even the parson. But what hope had he of that, and him the eldest of ten and his dad a stonebreaker? Never had a chance, your Dad didn't.'

Mam didn't seem to know anybody who had had a chance – not in Stratford Street. She was going to see to it that Mary did. Mam was sure that if she worked hard at school and behaved herself, she could get to be a teacher and be well off – the only chance a lass had of that, she said.

Mam went on, 'Mind you, everyone respects your Dad. And that's the most important thing of all, and don't you forget it, our Mary.'

Jinnie, who could mimic anyone, did Dad best of all. One day they were all outside the shop. Jinnie was sniffing, then blowing her nose like a trumpet on that awful old rag of hers. Dad, to the life, and no mistake! Even Mary had to laugh. Unfortunately, at that moment, Dad opened the glass door into the shop window to put in a new box of sherbet dabs.

The next thing they knew, Dad was at the door shaking his

fist and shouting, 'Wait till your Aunt Lizzie hears about this.' They all scattered, giggling, but Mary couldn't run away and she knew she'd be in trouble. It served her right, but it wasn't easy all the same: Dad and Jinnie really did make life complicated.

One day when Dad was at the flour bin in the darkest corner of the shop getting half a pound of flour for Jinnie, he turned round suddenly – 'I don't know what made me,' he said – and there was Jinnie with her hand in the big jar of pickled onions. He gave her a good talking to and charged her a ha'penny for the onion when he took the money for the flour.

'Oh, you shouldn't have,' Mam said. It was the first time Mary had ever heard her criticize him. 'You know what Lizzie will do to the poor lass.'

'Well, she deserves a good hiding: teach her not to go thieving again.'

'But it won't,' Mam said. 'That's not what the hiding'll be about, not if I know Lizzie. And we shouldn't leave things on the counter to tempt bairns, anyway.' Dad looked uncomfortable and he said no more.

After this Jinnie tormented him constantly. She seemed to know when it was Dad's turn to come into the shop from the back. She would open the shop door and then run off. Or, as things got worse, she would shout, 'How much are your rotten eggs today?' or 'Catching flies to put in the currants?' Rude things like that. Once she threw a shovelful of horse muck into the shop. But Mam had a word with her and she didn't do it again.

In the end Jinnie grew out of all this, but she was still 'bonny and impittent' Dad said, just the way she looked at him.

One day, a long time after the pickled onion affair, Mrs

Brooke's purse disappeared. Mrs Brooke was a Chapel friend who came every Friday for groceries. When she arrived she would give Dad her list and then go through to Mam for a cup of tea and some of the cake Mam had baked specially. She took the baby with her and left his pram in the shop. Dad would gather the groceries together and parcel them in best brown paper. Then he stayed in the shop weighing up sugar or tea or dried peas, so that the ladies could have their gossip, he said indulgently.

When it was time to go home to get her husband's tea ready, Mrs Brooke would come back into the shop, Mam holding the baby while Mrs Brooke got her purse out of the pram. Because it was far too big for her costume pocket, she always kept it under the pram cover. After Mrs Brooke had paid her bill, Dad would place the parcel at one end of the pram, and she'd put her purse back under the cover. It was quite a palaver: Mrs Brooke was their best customer and 'Chapel' as well.

Mary never met her except during school holidays, for Mrs Brooke always left before school was out. So on this particular day, Mary was surprised to see the pram still in the shop.

Dad wasn't there. He was in the back room with Mam and Mrs Brooke. They were all looking upset and Mrs Brooke was red-nosed and sniffing into her hankie. Her purse was missing!

Dad hadn't been out of the shop. She must have left her purse at Banks' on the High Street on the way here, Dad was saying, obviously not for the first time. No, Mrs Brooke said, she distinctly remembered putting it back in the pram. Mam looked anxious and made soothing sounds at the baby.

Mrs Brooke's tears began to flow again. No wonder: there'd been two pounds in that purse, or near enough.

Sometimes Dad's takings for a whole day didn't amount to that much. The baby began to whimper.

'Well,' Dad said at last, 'it looks as if it's gone from here. And me in the shop all the time.' He took a deep breath – two pounds was more to him than Mrs Brooke, most likely, for Mr Brooke was a foreman at Swan's shipyard, with an upstanding wage. 'So it's my responsibility.' He went to the sideboard and took two pound notes out of the money drawer.

'Oh no,' said Mrs Brooke. 'I couldn't. I should never have left it in the pram in the first place.' She was a very decent woman, as Mam and Dad agreed afterwards.

In the end, it was settled by Mrs Brooke not taking the money and Dad saying they would forget about the bill, which came to just over a pound. If the purse did turn up at Banks', Mr Brooke would come along and pay the bill even before he'd washed, never mind had his tea.

'It was that Jinnie,' Dad said, the minute Mrs Brooke had left. But Jinnie was at school, Mam objected. No she wasn't, Dad said. Lizzie had kept her away again. While Mrs Brooke was with Mam, Jinnie had come in for a gill of vinegar. The vinegar barrel was on the floor in the corner. Bending down, measuring out the vinegar and funnelling it into Jinnie's jug had taken some time. 'It was Jinnie right enough.' He even remembered that Jinnie was wearing an old jacket of her Grandad's. With big pockets.

'Well, we'll never know, not for sure,' Mam said, not wanting to believe it, and she began clearing away the tea-cups.

The next night, Saturday, Lizzie and her new husband went off as usual to the Crown and Anchor. Lizzie was wearing a brand-new hat. Stratford Street was full of it. New hats were something to talk about in 1926, what with pitmen threatened with pay-cuts, a strike looming up and the ship-yards laying men off.

'That proves it – it *was* Jinnie,' Dad said, when he heard about the hat. Mam didn't put up much of an argument. She did say, though, that Lizzie's man hadn't been laid off yet.

When all this happened, Mary hadn't seen much of Jinnie for ages. She was eleven now and working hard. She knew by this time that if you were a girl in Stratford Street there were only three things for you to do when you grew up. Stay an old maid, never have a place of your own, and be scoffed at behind your back. Or get married and never do anything except scour and polish, peel potatoes, wash dishes, poss and scrub clothes and argue about a space in the back lane to put out your clothes-line. Or be a servant, which was as bad as being a mam.

But there *was* one more thing you could be: a teacher. Then you would have a house of your own and a maid, Sunday clothes every day and real holidays, not just a day trip once a year to Tynemouth sands. Mam didn't know anybody who'd managed it, but she still believed it was Mary's best chance.

So Mary had to win a scholarship to the Secondary School at the other end of town. That would give her her chance. Her Headmistress, Miss Cheeseman, had chosen her and four others to put in for the exam, and she was giving them extra sums every afternoon when the rest of the class was doing needlework. And homework every night: more sums and compositions to do, spellings and general knowledge to learn. Mary felt quite sick with worry sometimes: she *had* to get a scholarship and there were only ten for all the girls in the town.

Then, with only a week to go to the exam, Miss Cheeseman sent for her. The class looked at her sympathetically.

Being sent for was never a good thing. When Mary came back with a letter for Mam in her hand, even Alice Bowes, her arch-rival for a scholarship, looked sorry. Mary hardly noticed. She could only worry about the letter. It had to be about the exam. Miss Cheeseman wasn't going to let her take the exam. Because of those blots and smudges on last week's test-paper, when someone had stuffed blotting-paper in her inkwell, Miss Cheeseman had been so vexed she had told Mary she would never win a scholarship if her work was like that on the real day. And she'd have to think whether she'd allow Mary to take the exam even.

At dinner time Mary ran all the way home: better know the worst straightaway. But the letter only asked Mam to go and see Miss Cheeseman at 4.15 that day, or the next if more convenient.

'Now what've you been up to, our Mary?' Dad asked.

'Don't go upsetting the bairn,' Mam said. 'It can't be anything much.' But she sounded worried. 'Eat up your dinner, there's a good lass. You need all the fish you can get. We want your brain in good fettle for the exam, now don't we?'

Mary liked fish, but today it just went round and round in her mouth and she could hardly get it down.

The afternoon seemed never-ending. On her way home she passed Mam in her Chapel clothes: navy costume, kid gloves, straw hat with shiny red cherries bobbing over the brim. Mam, she noticed, was sucking hard at a black bullet, so *she* was worried as well. But she only said, 'Set the tea-table, will you, there's a good lass.'

Mary set the table first job. She couldn't even think about homework so she went out, 'to play' she told Dad, but really to watch for Mam's return. Her friends – Jinnie wasn't among them – were playing 'Raspberry, Strawberry, Marmalade, Jam'. It had been Mary's favourite game last skipping season. It was all about getting married and who to. Now it seemed silly. Come to think about it, a lot of games were. Still, she hadn't anything better to do and at least she'd see Mam the minute she came into the street.

When it was her turn, the rope stopped first at 'thief', then at 'rags'. The other girls didn't know where to put themselves for laughing. Last year Mary would have laughed as well. Now she only pretended: it wasn't funny, more like a bad sign.

Then she saw Mam turning the corner. 'There's me Mam,' she said. 'I'll have to go in now.'

But Mam told her to finish the game and in her voice was, 'Don't you argue, our Mary.' And she looked sad. Mary's heart sank as she went to take her turn with the rope.

It wasn't long before the five o'clock buzzer at the ship-yard started bellowing. In a minute or two, men on bicycles would come racing along the street, running to trams on the High Street, or just hurrying home. Not so many nowadays but enough to stop the game. It was tea-time. She could go in now. She swallowed hard as she pushed open the shop door.

Mam, in ordinary blouse and skirt again, still looked serious, but not about the scholarship or untidy work. It was about Jinnie. Jinnie seemed to look up to Mam, Miss Cheeseman had said, so when her guardian had ignored her letters, Miss Cheeseman had written to Mam. Guardian? Surely guardians were only in books about posh people. Or else those men who gave food tickets to poor folk. So what was Miss Cheeseman on about?

'She meant Aunt Lizzie,' Mam was saying. 'You'd laugh if you didn't want to cry at the idea of Lizzie being that poor bairn's guardian. Miss Cheeseman thinks Aunt Lizzie may have put Jinnie up to her roguery. I had to say she could well be right.' Mam wrinkled her brow. 'You remember Mrs

Brooke's purse? Well, Jinnie *did* steal it. The only thing she was sorry about, Miss Cheeseman said.'

Mary couldn't see what Mrs Brooke's purse had to do with the Headmistress.

But Miss Cheeseman also told Mam there had been a number of thefts from the Teachers' Room. 'Phew, the nerve of it,' Dad said. Jinnie and two or three others had been suspected. Miss Cheeseman had marked some coins and left them in her coat pocket. Sure enough, they were stolen – by Jinnie. She owned up. Not that she could do anything else: the money was in that 'awful rag she called her handkerchief'. Actually she called it her snot-rag, Mary silently corrected the Headmistress.

Miss Cheeseman had put the fear of God into Jinnie. 'I didn't think anybody could do that,' Dad said. Mary knew that Miss Cheeseman could put the fear of God into *anybody*. All the same, although Miss Cheeseman was sure she had been responsible for thefts elsewhere, Jinnie hadn't owned up to any. Except Mrs Brooke's purse, which Miss Cheeseman hadn't even known about. And it was the only thing that seemed to worry Jinnie. 'Because of me, poor lass, would you believe it?' Mam said sadly. 'Miss Cheeseman's not going to call the police in this time. She sees now that the bairn's never had a chance. But I'm afraid Jinnie's in for it tomorrow – the strap in front of the whole school.'

'Serves her right. She's fourteen, old enough to know better.' Dad still didn't like Jinnie.

'Who was there ever to show her what was better?' Mam asked. 'I can't think what'll become of her. Getting married to a decent lad's her best chance but that'd not suit Lizzie. And how's she ever going to get a job? Miss Cheeseman will never give her a character now. And she's such a good lass at heart. And that bonny if she wasn't so neglected – the more's the pity.' A pity? Mary wished *she* was as bonny. 'Whatever's going to become of her?' Mam said again.

They never knew, at least not for a long time. Jinnie left school that same summer. Not long after, word went round Stratford Street that she'd disappeared. There'd been an awful row with Aunt Lizzie. Mrs Charlton Upstairs heard it. Aunt Lizzie didn't say much, only that Jinnie would be back, they'd see. She didn't even tell Jinnie's mother straightaway. She had to in the end, however, because Jinnie didn't come back.

Mary was eighteen and had started at Armstrong College in Newcastle, well on her way to becoming a teacher, when one day – it began like any other day – a car drove into Stratford Street. It caused a stir, as Mam told Mary that night. Although a lot of cars went along the street now, only the doctor's ever stopped. But this one did – at Aunt Lizzie's door. Mrs Charlton Upstairs, sitting at her open window as usual, must have just about fallen out, stretching to see who got out of the car.

It was Jinnie.

As if the car wasn't enough, Mrs Charlton had said, she was dressed up to the nines. 'A fur coat, none of your rabbit neither. And silk stockings. And her shoes – you should have seen them – she didn't get them for five shillings nor fifteen neither. And the parcels she fetched, and all in Fenwick's fancy paper. Didn't stay long, though. You'd wonder why she bothered, wouldn't you?'

'Poor Jinnie,' Mam said to Mary. 'Poor little lass.'

Now Mary knew what Mam meant. Jinnie, too, had found her chance.

Barker

PETER DICKINSON

THERE was a rich old woman called Mrs Barker who lived in a pokey little house at the top of a street so steep that it had steps instead of pavements. Mrs Barker could look all the way down the street from her windows and watch people puffing up the steps to bring her presents. Quite a lot of people did that, because Mrs Barker didn't have any sons or daughters or nieces or nephews, only what she called 'sort-ofs'. Sort-of-nieces, sort-of-nephews, sort-of-cousins and so on.

You want an example? Mr Cyril Blounder's mother's father's father's mother's sister had married Mrs Barker's father's mother's brother. That made Mr Blounder a very sort-of sort-of, but it didn't stop him bringing Mrs Barker lettuces from his garden and hoping that one day she'd die and leave him some money in her will. When he came Mrs

Barker's maid Hannah would bring him camomile tea, which he pretended to like, while Mrs Barker looked in the lettuces for slugs.

Most of the other sort-ofs did much the same, and they always got given camomile tea, and they all pretended to like it, because of the will. When they left, Mrs Barker would stand at her window and watch them go muttering down the hill. *She* knew what they were thinking.

Whenever a new sort-of was born Mrs Barker always sent a silver napkin-ring for a christening present, with a name on it. She chose the name herself, without asking the parents, so that was what the child got called. The parents usually decided it was worth it, because of the will. Mrs Barker preferred what she called 'sensible names'. She wrote them down in the back of her notebook to make sure she didn't choose the same one twice.

After that Mrs Barker paid no attention to the child until it was eight years old. Then she used to send a message inviting it to tea. So the parents would dress the child in its smartest clothes and take it up the steps, reminding it several times on the way to say 'Please' and 'Thank you' and not to make faces when it drank the camomile tea. (Some parents used to give their children camomile tea for a week before the visit, for practice.)

But more important than any of that advice was that when Mrs Barker asked the child what it wanted for a present it must choose something *really worth having*.

Because whatever it wanted, it got.

It was very extraordinary. Mrs Barker wasn't at all generous in other ways. She sent the most miserable mingy presents to the sort-ofs at Christmas, when they all bought her beautiful things they couldn't really afford, but just this once in their lives . . .

She would peer at each child with sharp little eyes and croak in her sour old voice, 'Well, what would you like for a present?' And the child would open its eyes as wide as it could and say a racing-bike *please* or a pony *please* or a huge model railway lay-out *please* ... Mrs Barker would write the request down in her notebook and put it away, but when the child was gone she would take out the notebook and cross off one of the names in the back.

A few days later the present would come, and it would be the best you could buy – the bike with the most gears, the briskest little pony, the most complicated railway set. But it would be the last good present that child ever got from Mrs Barker.

All this went on for years and years, until there were sort-ofs who'd been to tea with Mrs Barker when *they* were eight, now taking their own children up the steps and telling them to say please and thank you and above all to choose a present *really worth having* ...

One of these later sort-ofs was called Molly. (Her parents had hoped to call her Claudinetta, but it said Molly on her ring.) She was taken up the steps wearing a pink bow in her hair and a pale blue frock with a white lacy apron crackling new, and told all the usual things. Hannah opened the door for her and asked the parents to be back at half past five, and Molly went in alone.

As soon as the door was shut, Molly undid the ribbon in her hair and took off the lacy apron and put them on a chair in the hall before she went into Mrs Barker's parlour and shook hands. Mrs Barker's hand was cold and dry, with loose slithery skin. She pursed her purple lips and peered at Molly.

'You were wearing a pink bow when you came up the steps,' she said.

'I took it off,' said Molly.

Mrs Barker puffed out her cheeks like a frog, but didn't say anything. Hannah brought in the tea, thin little sandwiches, tiny dry cakes and a steaming teapot.

'Do you like camomile tea?' she asked.

'Not much, thank you, but I'll drink it if you want me to.'

Mrs Barker puffed out her cheeks again and peered at Molly, craning her neck like an old tortoise.

'What do you drink at home?' she said.

'Milk. Or orange juice. Or just water.'

Mrs Barker tinkled a small glass bell and when Hannah came she told her to bring Molly a glass of milk. After that they ate tea. Then they played an old-fashioned card-game. Then they did a jigsaw. And then Mrs Barker glanced out of the window and said, 'I can see your father coming up the steps. It is time for you to go. Would you like me to put the bow back in your hair?'

Molly ran and fetched the ribbon and apron and Mrs Barker tied them with trembling old fingers.

'Now,' she said, 'I expect you would like a present.'

Molly had been meaning to ask for a record-player, though she hadn't felt comfortable about it. Her parents had been so eager, so excited about the idea of a present *really worth having*, and now there was something strange in Mrs Barker's dry old voice, as though she was getting herself ready for a disappointment . . .

So without thinking Molly said what she'd felt all along.

'I don't think people should give each other presents till they know each other properly.'

Mrs Barker puffed out her cheeks.

'Very well,' she said.

'Thank you all the same,' said Molly. 'And thank you for the tea.'

Then her father knocked on the door and took her home.

Naturally her family wanted to know what she'd chosen for a present, and when she said nothing they didn't believe her. But nothing came and nothing came and they were furious, while all the other sort-ofs were filled with glee. (None of the sort-of families liked each other much, but that didn't stop them passing the gossip round.)

Then, several weeks later, a message came that Mrs Barker would like Molly to come to tea again, and she was not to dress up specially. This time there were hot buttered scones and fresh chocolate cake and not a whiff of camomile tea anywhere. But nothing was said about presents.

The same thing happened a few weeks later, and a few weeks later still. Now Molly's family was filled with glee and all the other sort-ofs were furious. None of their children had ever been asked to a second tea, so it was obvious Mrs Barker had decided at last who was going to get her money, and now it was too late to tell the children the trick was not to ask the old so-and-so for anything at all.

This went on till almost Christmas, when a letter came.

My dear Molly,

I believe you and I may by now be said to know each other properly, so it is time we exchanged presents. You told me on your last visit that your family dog was about to have puppies. Would you choose one for me, and I shall send you something on Christmas Day.

Yours affctntly,
Ethelswitha Barker

The family dog was a mongrel, and nobody could guess who the father of her last litter might be. Molly's parents wanted to sneak off and buy a beautiful pedigree pup and pretend it came from the litter, but Molly said Mrs Barker was much too sharp not to spot that. She chose a black-and-white male and took it up the hill to show Mrs Barker, who said Molly was to take it home and look after it till it was house-trained. She added that it was to be called Barker. (A sure sign, most of the sort-ofs thought, that she was losing her wits. Naming a dog after your dead husband – honestly!)

Molly's Christmas present turned out to be a yellow waterproof hat and coat and a pair of blue wellies – for taking Barker for walks in wet weather, the note that came with them said.

When he was house-trained Barker went to live with Mrs Barker, and Molly would go most days to take him for a walk. Sometimes she stayed for tea, sometimes not. Time passed. More sort-ofs climbed the hill for their first tea. If they asked for presents they got them, and if they didn't Mrs Barker sent a cheque and note telling the parents to buy something the child needed.

Then people noticed that the writing on the notes was getting shaky. Next they saw the doctor going up the steps to the pokey little house three times in one week. Then an ambulance came. Soon after that Mrs Barker died. All this while Molly took Barker for walks, as usual.

All the sort-ofs were invited to hear the will read. They came, grinding their teeth, except for Molly's parents who did their best not to look too triumphant, though they'd already decided on the grand house outside the town which Molly was going to buy with her money. It had a lovely big garden for her to run about in.

By the time the lawyer had finished reading the will *everybody* was grinding their teeth.

Mrs Barker had left some money to Hannah, enough for her to retire and be comfortable. That wasn't too bad. But then she had left the rest, the whole lot, an enormous amount, to Barker!

And they weren't even going to get their hands on it when Barker died. After that it was going to charity. Until then it was all Barker's. Molly was to be Barker's guardian. There was a lot of legal language, with trustees and heaven knows what, but what it all meant was that Molly was the only person who knew what Barker wanted. If she said Barker was to have something, he was to get it. If not, the money stayed in the bank. And provided Barker lived till Molly was sixteen, she was the one who was going to choose the charities which got the money in the end.

Some of the sort-ofs talked about going to law to have the will altered, but the lawyers said it was all very carefully drawn up and in any case no one could be sure who would get the money if they did get the will changed – it would probably have gone straight to the charities. So they decided to put up with it.

Almost at once Molly's parents realized this mightn't be too bad, after all. Barker needed a big garden to run about in, didn't he, and it happened there was this suitable house outside the town . . .

Molly said she'd go and see what Barker thought (though really she spent most of the time talking to Hannah). When she came back she said Barker wanted to stay in his own home, with Hannah to look after him, and Hannah didn't mind. (It was her home too – she'd lived there since she was sixteen.)

Molly's parents were *not* pleased and there was a real row, but Molly stuck to her guns. She kept saying Barker had made up his mind. Her father stormed off to the lawyers next morning, but they said the same thing. It was absolutely clear. If Molly said Barker wanted to stay in his own house, that was that. You may think it was tough-minded of Molly to stick it out, but she was a tough-minded girl. Perhaps that was why Mrs Barker had chosen her.

And she had something to help her. On the day the will had been read one of the lawyers had given her a letter and told her she wasn't to show it to anyone else. He hadn't even read it himself. It said:

My dear Molly,

You will now know the contents of my will. It is no doubt very selfish of me to amuse myself in this manner, but I am a selfish old person and that's that. When I was young I inherited a ridiculous amount of money, but it was all tied up in Trusts until I was twenty-five, so I got no fun out of it when I was a child. I have always resented this.

I see no reason why any of my connections should inherit my money. It will do far more good if it goes to charity, but it amuses me to think that before that a child might have some fun spending a little of it, as I never did. That is why I devised a little test to choose a child who was likely to be level-headed about money. I am glad it was you who passed the test.

If I were to leave the money to you till you are of age, people would insist on it being spent 'for your own good', and you would have very little say in the matter. That is why I have left it to Barker. My will says you are to be his guardian, but really it is the other way about. He is there to protect you – you are quite clever enough to see how useful he will be in this role. I strongly advise you to establish the point at the earliest possible moment.

Barker is an earnest soul (as I am not), and I think he will make a very good guardian.

Yours affctntly,
Ethelswitha Barker

So Molly did what the letter suggested and 'established the point'. She liked their own home, and so did her parents, really. The other one was much too grand for them, and after a few weeks her parents began to think so too.

But soon the other sort-ofs realized that Molly's family weren't the only ones who could suggest things Barker might like. They would stop Molly while she was taking him for one of his walks and say he looked a bit off-colour, and wouldn't a bit of sea-air do him good? Now it happened there was this holiday villa in Cornwall, a real snip, though he wouldn't want to use it all the time, would he, and maybe when he wasn't there it would be best if one of the Frossetts (or the McSniggs, or the Blounders, or the Globotzikoffs, or whichever of the sort-of families had thought of the scheme), went and took care of the place. For a suitable fee, perhaps.

Molly said Barker would think it over. The following week, she explained Barker thought he'd like to go on a rabbiting holiday this year, with Molly, of course, but he didn't want her to be lonely so she'd better bring a few friends and her Mum and Dad to drive him about to good rabbiting places. Barker paid for the petrol and the hotel rooms.

A bit later a new baby sort-of was born and had to be christened. Barker sent a silver napkin-ring, but without a name on it. Privately Molly wondered what would have happened if she'd told the silversmith to put 'Bonzo', but she explained that Barker didn't think it was quite right for a dog to tell people what to call their children.

And then one day in the supermarket Molly heard two mothers of sort-of families chatting about the old days, and the excitement of taking their children up to have tea with Mrs Barker, and thinking of *really worthwhile* presents, and wondering whether by any chance little Sam or Betsy would be the one . . .

Molly talked to Barker about it on their next walk, and the upshot was that the notes started coming again, inviting the children to tea when it was their turn. It was a bit different, because Barker didn't ask questions the way Mrs Barker used to, and the food was better, and there was Molly to talk to and play with, but there was always camomile tea (or that's what Molly said it was, though it didn't taste much different from ordinary tea).

In fact it all became rather like an old custom, which people have forgotten the reason for, but go on doing because they've always done it and it's a bit picturesque and so on. And there were the presents, of course. They were as good as ever, but somehow it didn't seem quite so mean and grabby asking for them, which is what most people, in their heart of hearts, had probably felt, just as Molly had. And nobody now thought that Barker was going to leave all his money to a child who said 'Please' and 'Thank you' properly or an adult who turned up on the doorstep with a particularly nice present.

Mr Cyril Blounder, quite early on, did climb the steps one day with a bone he swore he'd dug up in his allotment, though it looked remarkably fresh. Hannah gave him camomile tea on the doorstep, and all the other sort-ofs felt he'd made a fool of himself and nobody else tried it.

Time passed. Nothing much new happened. Molly got older, and so did Barker. You'd have thought he was rather a dull dog if you met him, but he had interesting ideas. He longed to travel, Molly said, but he couldn't because of the quarantine, so instead he used to send Hannah and her sister who lived somewhere up in the North on annual holidays to exciting places, and Hannah would come back and show him her slides. He gave generously to charities on flag-days – not only to the RSPCA – and took a keen interest in nature preservation. He had some handsome trees planted in the park, with a bench under them which said:

IN FOND MEMORY OF ETHELSWITHA BARKER
Loving Mistress

Strangers didn't know quite what to make of that, but none of the local people thought it odd.

In fact one year there was a proposal to have Barker elected Mayor. It was only half-serious, of course, but it worried the real parties enough to pay lawyers to find out whether you can elect a dog mayor, which you can't. But he might have got in. For a dull dog, he was surprisingly popular.

One lucky result from Barker's point of view was that he got quite an active love-life. In a town like that most people had pedigree dogs and used to send the bitches off to be mated. They tried to shoo mongrels away when their bitches were on heat, but it almost became a sort of status symbol to let your bitch have one litter of Barker's pups, so after a few years there were quite a lot of his children in the town – Barker's own sort-ofs. They weren't sort-ofs because their relationship with him was complicated, like Mrs Barker's had been. He was their father and they were his children. That was usually clear from the black-and-white patches. They were sort-of collies and sort-of Labradors and sort-of dachshunds and so on.

Curiously, people didn't mind having these mongrels born to their prize bitches, and even more curiously this wasn't because Barker was so rich – he didn't send the family a huge present when it happened, only the right number of collars, with names for the puppies on them. It was because the whole town was proud of having him around. He was odd, and different, and when nothing much was happening in the world reporters would come and write stories for their newspapers about him.

Of course they never got it quite right – reporters don't. It was difficult for them to understand the difference it made, all that money belonging to a dog, and not a person. When old Mrs Barker had been alive people used to think about her money a lot, envying her or scheming how to wheedle cash out of her, or complaining about her not spending it on things they thought important. But somehow when the money belonged to a dog it stopped being so serious. There were still schemes and complaints, of course (you don't change people *that* much), but whoever was listening to the schemer or complainer was always likely to switch the conversation into jokes about Barker, almost as though the money wasn't real. It was, of course – it got trees planted and the spire repaired and it endowed nature trails and sent the over-60s on coach trips and bought a site for the Youth Club – but it didn't *matter* the way it had seemed to before. Even the sort-of families stopped being as spiteful about each other as they used to be – the money was out of everyone's reach now, so there wasn't much point.

Dogs don't live as long as humans, so it wasn't long before people started to fuss about Barker's health, and knit coats for him to wear in the winter – though he had a perfectly good thick coat of his own – and speak sharply to delivery-men who hurtled round corners in their vans. Barker was a fool about traffic. Of course Hannah was supposed to keep him locked in and Molly always fastened his lead when they were walking anywhere near roads, but if he saw a cat or smelt a rabbit there was absolutely no holding him, or he'd manage to slip out on one of his love-affairs while Hannah had the door open to take in the milk. The Town Council had notices put up at the most dangerous places, saying CAUTION: DOG CROSSING, but they weren't much use as Barker never crossed twice in the same place.

Still, he bore a charmed life for eight years. He had lots of narrow escapes. Strangers driving through sometimes hit lampposts or traffic islands trying to avoid him, and they couldn't understand why everybody was furious with *them*, and why there were always a dozen witnesses ready to come forward saying it was *their* fault.

The over-60s coach got him in the end – coming back from a trip Barker had paid for himself. Molly said that Barker had always wanted a really good send-off, so there was a jolly funeral with masses to eat and drink for the whole town, and a fun-fair and fireworks.

After that Molly spent a whole week with the lawyers, organizing which charities should get Barker's money. Practically all of it went to ordinary sensible places, a bit to the RSPCA of course, but mostly things like Cancer Research and War on Want. But Molly kept one per cent aside (that doesn't sound very much, but Mrs Barker really had been enormously rich, so it was still a useful amount) for a special charity she had set up. The lawyers had had a lot of trouble making it legal, but she'd insisted it was what Barker wanted, so they managed it somehow.

That was why all the families in the town which had one of Barker's puppies as their pet got a surprise cheque through the letter box, with a letter saying it was to be spent exclusively for the benefit of their dog, and the youngest person in the house was the only one who could say what that dog wanted.

It was an idea that would have amused Mrs Barker, Molly thought, and made her wrinkle her lips into her sour little smile – sort-ofs getting something in the end. Only not her sort-ofs. Barker's.

The Fat Wizard

DIANA WYNNE JONES

THE Fat Wizard lived up at the Big House in our village and he always opened the Church Fête. As well as being very fat, he had a purple face and pop eyes and a grey bristly beard. He despised everyone. When he opened the Fête, he said things like, 'This Fête gets more boring every year. Why do you silly people love it?' This was considered very witty, because the Fat Wizard was rich. I preferred Mrs Ward's cousin Old Ned, myself. Everyone despised Old Ned, but at least he went mad in the church porch every full moon. The Fat Wizard never did anything but grumble.

My Auntie May always went to the Church Fête, although we were Chapel. She went for the jumble. Auntie May was the most respectable witch I have ever known and she did not like Chapel people to know she bought cast-off clothes.

She lived in the house on the corner opposite the White Horse and everything indoors was just so. I came to live in that house as soon as I left school, to train to be Auntie May's assistant.

Auntie May used to look through her lace curtains and count how often Mrs Ward went into the pub. 'Look at her!' she would snort. 'Red dress, hung all over with jewellery, and enough make-up to sink a battleship!' Though they were both witches, Auntie May and Mrs Ward were opposites in every way. Auntie May was tall and lean and dour, and she wore dour brown clothes. Mrs Ward was small and glamorous, and she had lovely legs. I used to admire Mrs Ward and wish I was her assistant, not Auntie May's.

Anyway, the Church Fête was only two days away. Auntie May and I were talking about it while I cleared away breakfast.

'And you're not to bowl for the pig this year, Cheryl,' Auntie May was saying, when there was a sort of *boom* and a flash. The Fat Wizard's manservant George appeared in the middle of the kitchen.

'The Wizard wants to see you at once,' George said.

Really it was a wonder I didn't drop the teapot! Everyone said George was really a demon, but I didn't think even demons had a right to appear in people's kitchens like that.

Auntie May took it quite calmly. 'What does he want?' she said. But George only vanished, with another boom and a flash. 'Well, we'd better go,' Auntie May said, getting her flat brown hat off its peg and pinning it bolt upright across her head.

So off we went, with me wondering what gave the Fat Wizard the right to order us about. As we passed the Vicarage and came to the church, I was wishing for about the thousandth time that I could go and live in Town. The Vicar was trying to chase my pig Ranger out of the churchyard.

'About that pig,' Auntie May said forbiddingly.

'I won't do it again,' I said guiltily, as we turned into the drive of the Big House. I'd won Ranger at the Church Fête last year, you see, and I'm pretty sure I won him by unfair use of magic. You know how it is, when you're willing and willing for the skittles to fall over. I went a bit far in my willing, and I'm pretty sure half the skittles went over without my bowls even touching them. I was given this squealing, struggling, long-legged piglet, and there was only my mother's tiny backyard to keep him in. He kept getting out. At first, people in the village kept catching him and bringing him back. But he got cleverer and cleverer, until everyone gave up. By now Ranger was a large white amiable pig, and you were likely to meet him anywhere.

The Vicar was still shouting at Ranger as we came to the Big House. George opened the tradesmen's door to us. 'Took your time, didn't you?' he said, and he led the way down a corridor, waggling his rump as he walked. I think he waggled because he was allowing for a tail, and he didn't have a tail in human form. But he shocked Auntie May. She whispered to me not to look.

The Fat Wizard was in a sunny morning-room having breakfast. When we came in, he was scraping up the last of a quart tub of fat-free yoghurt. Then he poured a pint of milk on a hill of branflakes, emptied the sugar bowl over it and ate most of that before he looked up. 'Here at last, are you, May?' he grunted. He didn't notice me.

'What can we do for you, sir?' Auntie May asked.

The Fat Wizard guzzled up the rest of his branflakes. Then he cut a giant slice off a starch-reduced loaf. He spread that with most of a packet of slimmers' magarine and ladled marmalade on top of that. 'The doctors say I'm too fat,' he said peevishly. 'They make me eat this chicken-feed all the time, but it's not doing a scrap of good. I've *got* to lose weight. Make me up a potion that will do the trick.'

'Of course, sir,' Auntie May said politely. 'But couldn't you do that yourself, sir?'

The Fat Wizard tipped the rest of the jar of marmalade on his bread and ate it in two bites. 'Potions are not men's work,' he said with his mouth full. 'Go away, woman, and mix me a weight-reducing potion, and get it here today, or I'll get Tallulah Ward to do it.'

Rude old man! We hurried home, and Auntie May did her best for him, but it is not easy to set that kind of spell quickly, even when she had me to grind up the ingredients for her. We worked hard the rest of the day. We were straining the mixture all evening, and we only had it bottled just before midnight.

'Take it round to him, Cheryl,' Auntie May said, breathlessly slapping a label on the bottle. 'And run!'

I supposed Auntie May could not bear the thought of Mrs Ward being asked to do the potion. I took the bottle and set off down the street at a trot, with the bottle foaming and fizzing eerily in my fist. It was quite dark, and I was scared. When I turned in at the gate of the Big House, a large white shape drifted across the drive in front of me. I was too scared even to scream. I just stood.

Then the moon came up over the Fat Wizard's chimneys and the white shape said 'Honk!', and I realized it was only Ranger. He knew it was me. He came and brushed his bristly self against me.

'Yes, you're a nice pig,' I said. 'Much nicer than the Fat Wizard. But don't ever do that again!'

Then I went on and George tried to scare me too. He appeared suddenly in a red light, outside the front door. But I had used up all my fright on Ranger. I held the bottle scornfully out to him. George snatched it. Then he turned and went in through the front door without opening it first, waggling his stern as he melted through it.

I was annoyed, and I could hear Ranger grunting and foraging among the trees as I went back down the drive, so I was not particularly frightened until I got to the gate. Then midnight struck. Something howled, like a dog, but not quite like, over in the churchyard. My hair tried to stand on end, until I realized that it was full moon and the noise was only Old Ned, going mad as usual. I went across the road to have a look.

This is something all the village children like to do. There was a whole row of them sitting on the churchyard wall, ready to watch Old Ned. The biggest was Lizzie Holgate's eldest boy, Jimmy, from the council houses. Jimmy said, 'We've been feeding your pig all this week.'

'Thanks,' I said.

'He's a good animal,' Jimmy said. 'I like a pig with brains.'

'Shut up!' someone else whispered. 'Old Ned's starting.'

Old Ned came crawling out of the church porch on all fours. That was how he always began. He thought he was a wolf. But I still don't know why they called him *Old* Ned. There was no grey in his hair. When he felt the moonlight across his face, he stood up and stretched both arms in the air.

'Silver temptress!' he shouted. 'Take this spell off me!'

We giggled a bit and waited for what he would say next. He can go on for hours. He came shambling down the path between the graves, staring. 'I see you!' he yelled. 'I see you, Cheryl Watson!'

And he was staring straight at me. I could feel the row of boys moving away from me. Nobody dared be with anyone Old Ned noticed at full moon.

'I see you, Cheryl,' said Old Ned. 'My mistress tells you to make sure to spend tomorrow night at your mother's house. It will be to your advantage.' He gave a mad laugh and went shambling back into the church porch.

'The show's over,' Jimmy said to the others. They all got off the wall and ran away without speaking to me. I didn't think the show *was* over. Old Ned began howling again as I went back to Auntie May's, but none of us felt like staying. I kept wondering. I woke up next morning still wondering why Old Ned had noticed me.

But that went out of my head when Mrs Ward came banging on Auntie May's door. Auntie May glared at her. Mrs Ward had her hair in a pink turban and her red coat on over what looked to be a frilly nightdress. Tears were driving black streaks down her make-up.

'Oh, what *have* you gone and done to our poor Fat Wizard!' she gasped. She was killing herself laughing. 'Come and take a look!'

We ran outside. Most of the village was out there, either in a row in front of the White Horse or up in the churchyard. And there was George, frantically running up the street with a coil of rope, trying to throw a loop of rope over the Fat Wizard. The Fat Wizard was floating and bobbing about forty feet over everyone's heads. You could see he was nearly as light as air. And he was *livid*. He was wearing purple pyjamas and his face was the same colour. His eyes were blue bubbles of pure rage.

'Oh dear,' said Auntie May.

'It's not your fault,' I said. 'He asked you to reduce his weight.'

'Get me *down*, George!' the Fat Wizard bawled in a high windy voice.

George threw the rope again and hit him with the loop,

which made the Fat Wizard bob another ten feet up in the air. The wind caught him and whirled him towards the church.

'Help, George!' he yelled, bouncing against the steeple.

'Trying to, sir! Out of my way!' George shouted, leaping over gravestones and dodging among staring people. 'Oh, I do blame myself for opening the window without looking, sir!'

Another gust of wind sent the Fat Wizard slowly bumping and scraping up the steeple. Auntie May went indoors then and made me come too. She said the disgrace was too much. I couldn't see properly from her house. All I could see was Lizzie Holgate arriving, pushing her old pushchair with her twins in it, with Mary and Jimmy and Charlene carrying the smaller babies. I saw Lizzie take two of the babies and send Jimmy and Mary off, but I couldn't see *where*. Jimmy told me later.

The Fat Wizard was hooked on the weathercock by then. But of course George was a demon, so he couldn't touch the church. Lizzie sent Jimmy and Mary up the stairs inside the steeple with the rope. They climbed out at the top and tied the rope to him. Then they unhooked him and George hauled him down into the churchyard. Jimmy said the Fat Wizard didn't even thank them.

While that was happening, Mrs Ward ran past and went into her house, still laughing. Soon after, George came panting along with the rope over his shoulder, towing the bobbing, fluttering Fat Wizard like an angry barrage balloon. We had a good view, because Mrs Ward lived six houses up, beyond the place where the road bends round the White Horse. It took George twenty minutes to work the bouncing and bobbling Fat Wizard through Mrs Ward's front door.

'Well, she should have had time to get dressed by now – even the way *she* dresses,' Auntie May said viciously.

She was very upset. So was I, rather. It could have been my fault. I told you how I came to win Ranger in the heat of the moment. I *could* have put in a bit of ill-wishing when I grated the ingredients or when I handed the potion to George. That made me feel I ought to keep out of Auntie May's way for a while. I asked if I could go and see my mother.

Auntie May felt like being alone. She told me to stay the night if I wanted. 'But make sure to come back in time to go to the Fête tomorrow,' she added.

My mother lives out along Water Lane. It felt strange to be going there and not living there any more.

'Is someone blaming you for that weight-reducing spell?' my mother asked. She had heard all about it, of course.

'I'm not sure,' I said. 'Has there been anything to my advantage here?'

'Not that I know of,' said my mother.

'Then I'll have to stay the night,' I said.

Mother was not too keen on the idea. She turned out to be using my old room as an apple-store. But she is fond of me, and she let me spend the night on the sofa, which was much warmer than my old room. And in the morning, as if Old Ned had *known*, there was a letter from my Godmother. My Godmother is head of the biggest coven in Town. She wrote that I must be about old enough to be leaving school now, and she invited me to come and join her and train to be a witch.

'Write and tell her you can't,' said my mother. 'If I'd known she was going to offer, I'd never have let you go to May. But it's too late now. You can't let May down.'

'Bother!' I said sadly. I was longing to live in Town. I put the letter in my pocket to answer later and went back to Auntie May's.

I came back to a sight I had quite often seen before. Auntie May was standing dourly in the street, staring at her house. Most of the side wall was missing. The roof was sagging, and the front room was filled with broken laths, plaster and the ruins of Auntie May's furniture. The house is on a right-angled bend, you see. A lorry driver coming through the village in the night could see the White Horse, but not Auntie May's house on the other side of the street beyond it. This lorry driver had not turned his wheel quickly enough and had arrived in Auntie May's front room in the middle of the night. He had driven through my bedroom too. Almost the first thing I saw through the hole was the ruins of my bed, upside down in the plaster next to the street. My bedroom floor was missing. I gulped a bit when I saw and said a silent 'Thank you' to Old Ned.

'I am insured,' Auntie May said glumly. 'And I dare say I deserved it for getting that potion wrong.'

'You mean,' I said, 'the Fat Wizard?'

Auntie May said 'Hush!' and gave a stiff, uneasy look all round. 'Yes, this happens every time I cross him. Well, come in. The kitchen's still there.'

We picked our way through the rubble. I no longer wondered why Auntie May hurried to obey the Fat Wizard when he wanted something. And I was angry. The Fat Wizard had not even *thought* what might happen to me!

'They say he gave Tallulah Ward a gold bracelet,' Auntie May said bitterly, while the kettle boiled. 'She made him heavy again. I saw him walk past on his own two feet with that George fussing round him. Ah well, life is not meant to be fair. I mustn't grumble.'

I did not agree at all. I said, 'Didn't he give the Holgates anything?'

'Of course not!' Auntie May said, surprised at the idea.

I was still angry when we set off to the Church Fête that afternoon. We had to spend all morning putting No Entry spells on the house. The builder was too busy with the Fat Wizard's gutters to board up the hole. And my best dress was somewhere in the rubble under my bed. I only had my old jersey and skirt. The Church Fête, in spite of a chilly wind, was full of people in their summer best, and the first person we met when we went through the gate was Mrs Ward. She was wearing a new red dress and making her new gold bracelet chink up and down her arm by carrying a big bunch of magic balloons which kept tugging to get away. She smiled meanly at us.

'Come for your jumble, have you?' she said. 'I'm surprised you dare show your faces. You look just like the two fools you are.'

I'd admired Mrs Ward up to then. I was quite disillusioned. Auntie May went dark red and we both pretended not to hear. It was easy to pretend, because the loudspeakers were making sounds like a cat being attacked by bagpipes. We stalked past Mrs Ward.

Usually Auntie May waits near the jumble stall until the Fête is opened, so that she can be first there; but this time we stalked past the jumble, and the rifle range, and the lucky dip and then the bowls pitch. There was a small white piglet in a hutch to one side of the bowls. It kept pushing its snout through the chicken-netting and getting stuck.

'Now, Cheryl!' Auntie May said, seeing me looking.

But I could see the piglet was not clever like Ranger and I was not interested this year.

Ranger was there, of course. He came pushing through the

127

hedge as we were going to the flower tent. He gave me a friendly wink and trotted off into the crowd. A couple of ice-cream vans had arrived, and Ranger's plump white shape was here, there and everywhere, begging for ice-cream. Lizzie Holgate was there, handing money out in handfuls to all her six kids. All of them bought ice-creams with it and most of them gave theirs straight to Ranger. Auntie May snorted at the waste and we went round the flowers. The judges had already mysteriously been there and given First Prizes to all the wrong things. We stood in the hot, squashed grass looking at the Single Rose. Auntie May was feeling better by then.

'That, Cheryl,' she said, 'is the Way of Life. You have to accept it.'

The Fat Wizard had won with a scrawny yellow rose. Old Ned had put in a perfect and wonderful red rose and hadn't won a prize at all. I didn't feel at all like accepting it.

All this time, the Vicar's voice kept coming over the loud-speakers saying, 'One. Two. Three. Testing,' mixed with howls and squalls. As we came out of the tent, he said 'Ninety-nine!' followed by a noise like God eating celery and the band started to play outside the beer tent. The Fat Wizard's large shiny Bentley was bumping slowly across the field towards the Vicar. Auntie May and I got quickly to the back of the crowd.

'I'm sure CRUNCH CHOMP needs no introduction from THUNDERCRASH,' the loudspeakers said as the car stopped and George sprang out dressed as a chauffeur. 'We are delighted SQUASH welcome CLATTER once again to TEA-TRAYS RUN OVER BY LORRY our little Fête.'

George opened the door of the Bentley and the Fat Wizard climbed out. He was very angry again. He puffed and he glared and he panted, and he finally got both feet out on to the grass. They sank up to the ankles as soon as he took a step. The earth quivered. He took two more steps. Music stands in front of the band fell over. By this time the Fat Wizard was walking along a small trench, sinking lower every second. He must have weighed well over a ton. His bulging blue eyes flickered angrily about, looking for someone.

Auntie May said, in a mild, pleased voice, 'I hope Tallulah Ward has the sense to keep out of sight.'

But Mrs Ward was right near the edge of the crowd, easy to pick out by her red dress and the bunch of straining balloons. Her face was so pale that she had a bright red spot of make-up showing on each cheek.

Just then Lizzie Holgate came round the Bentley, pushing her pushchair and surrounded by all her kids. They seemed to be looking for a good place to stand. Jimmy and Mary had to lift the pushchair over the trench the Fat Wizard had made, so that for a second the whole family was milling round the Fat Wizard.

When they moved on again, the Fat Wizard was the right weight. He climbed easily out of his trench and he took an easy step or so. But it never occurred to him to thank the Holgates. He just glared at Mrs Ward.

'If you'll just come over to the microphone, sir —' the Vicar called.

But Ranger had followed the Holgates round the Bentley, hoping for more ice-cream. He saw something was going on and he stood, looking about inquisitively. He looked at the Fat Wizard.

'Ah!' said the Fat Wizard. 'Now I know what to do to that woman!' He pointed a fat finger at Mrs Ward, and he shouted out something that made an even louder noise than the loudspeakers.

All Mrs Ward's balloons went up together in a huddle, like

129

hair standing on end. In place of Mrs Ward, there was suddenly a thin white pig with blobs of pink on its cheeks. It ran about among everyone's legs, trying to get itself out of its red dress. Then it dashed into the beer tent, trailing underclothes and squealing, and there was suddenly a lot of noise from in there too.

Everyone except Ranger looked at the Vicar, and the Vicar looked at the sky. Ranger looked at me – in a puzzled, reproachful way, as if he thought it was my fault that Mrs Ward was knocking tables over and squealing in the beer tent.

'Where do I stand to open this silly Fête?!' the Fat Wizard said.

'Oh no you won't open the Fête!' I screamed. I couldn't bear the way Ranger was looking. I rushed through the crowd and I stood in the open, with one hand stretched out towards the Fat Wizard and the other stretched towards Ranger. 'You're selfish and greedy and cruel!' I yelled. '*Ranger* would make a better human than you!'

The loudspeakers made a MOTORBIKE-STARTING-IN-HEAVEN noise. After that, Ranger and the Fat Wizard seemed to have changed places. The Fat Wizard was standing where Ranger had been, staring at me with amused piggy eyes. Where the Fat Wizard had been was a very fat pig with a sort of black waistcoat marked on its white skin. This pig had blue eyes and it looked stunned.

Jimmy Holgate shouted, 'Cheryl! Look out!'

George was climbing out of the Bentley. His smart chauffeur's uniform burst off him. He leapt towards me, towering over me, huge and blue-black. The tail he always seemed to be missing was lashing round his legs, thick and hairy, with a forked tip. I was terrified.

Lizzie Holgate and her kids arrived beside me. Auntie

May was there too, holding her hat on dourly. And my mother was next to Auntie May, which *did* surprise me, because she never goes to the Church Fête. George towered and gnashed his long teeth. We all shouted '*Avaunt*!' and the loudspeakers went SCREAM POOP SCREAM and George vanished. The poor little piglet down by the bowling pitch suddenly went mad. George had possessed it. It screamed so hard that it almost drowned the noise in the beer tent.

Ranger winked at me. 'Let's get this Fête open,' he said to the Vicar in a pleasant grunty voice, 'and we can all have an ice-cream.'

But Lizzie Holgate was whispering to my mother, 'Can you send her somewhere where there's no pigs around?'

Mother caught the glaring blue eye of the pig with the waistcoat. 'Her Godmother. In Town,' she whispered back.

I caught the two-thirty bus outside the gate. While the bus was turning round, Old Ned let the piglet out of its hutch and it chased after the bus, foaming at the mouth, until Jimmy Holgate managed to catch it by one leg.

I have never dared go back. Mother writes that the blue-eyed pig with the waistcoat is still roaming the woods, but they sent George to the bacon factory some time ago. Mother has Mrs Ward in the sty in her backyard. Even the Holgates can't turn her back. Ranger is still living at the Big House. He opens the Church Fête every year, and Mother says you couldn't have a nicer landlord.

A Speck of Dust

PETER CARTER

BEYOND glittering skyscrapers, mine dumps caught the sun. In the long afternoon light they looked almost pretty, but from them fine dust was blowing across the rugby ground and a particle had got into the eye of Jan Vorster. It was painful and he was momentarily blinded. To a roar of dismay and derision, he fumbled a simple pass and dropped the ball. He tried to recover but was slammed aside by the opposing back, who scooped up the ball and scored a try which was converted. As the whistle then blew for time, instead of the Paul Kruger School winning by four points it lost by two, and to a very superior look-down-their-nose-at-you English school at that. And as the back had kicked Jan in the face it wasn't the best match he had ever played in. Indeed, as it was a Cup competition and this had been the semi-final, it was probably the worst match of his life.

In the showers the water was cold, but not as cold as the reception Jan got. Only two people spoke to him: his Captain who cursed, and the school coach, who did the same, adding that he would talk to Jan again on Monday – and he wasn't referring to a pleasant chat, either.

But, as if to make up for this, in the car going home Jan's father had plenty to say. 'Stupid!' he roared. 'Stupid! A perfect pass and you dropped it like a girl.'

'I had dust in my eye,' Jan mumbled.

'Dust in my –!' Mr Vorster shouted. 'You know what you've done? You've let the side down, that's what. Let the side down, let the school down, let me down! And in front of all those people! Ach! I couldn't look them in the eye. No wonder the country's going to rack and ruin –' He banged his horn at an old woman who was pushing a battered pram loaded with rubbish across the road. 'Black cow,' he muttered and fell into a sullen silence which lasted all the way home.

Home was a bungalow in an interminable road of bungalows backing on to a dreary park, each separate dwelling crouching behind a thorn hedge and each one bearing a huge burglar alarm. They climbed out of the car and went on to the veranda. Bok, their enormous ridgeback dog, came to meet them but Mr Vorster shoved him out of the way with his foot.

'Clear off,' he said. 'And you, too,' speaking over his shoulder to Jan. 'Get out of my sight.'

He went into the sitting-room, slamming the door behind him, and Jan slouched into the kitchen. Martha, the maid, was leaning over the stove. She turned as he entered, the warm smile on her face changing to consternation as she saw him.

'Aiee!' she cried. 'What have you been up to?'

Jan touched his face. It was numb, but under his finger-tips he could feel a lump which seemed as big as Table Mountain. 'I got kicked,' he said.

Martha peered at Jan's face. 'Kicked by a buffalo,' she said. '*Tss*, that rugby game, every week the same.'

'Not *every* week,' Jan said.

Martha waved the objection aside and ran a flannel under the cold-water tap. 'Sit down and put this on your face and I'll make you a cup of tea.'

Jan held the icy flannel to his face and sipped hot sweet tea through the side of his mouth.

'Where's Baas?' Martha asked.

Jan tilted his head. 'In there.'

'Not happy, hey?'

'No, he isn't.' Jan was rueful.

'Because you got hurt?'

Jan looked suspiciously at Martha. Just for one moment he wondered if she was making fun of him, but he dismissed the thought as it arrived. No black would ever dare make fun of a white – not in the Vorster household, anyway. Not that he and Martha hadn't had good times together in the long years she had worked for the Vorsters: playing when he had been bathed, on the swings in the park, and during the long hours he had spent in the kitchen, listening entranced as Martha had told him the Zulu tales of talking lizards and clever spiders of which she had a vast fund, although – and it had surprised Jan when he found it out – she had been born in Johannesburg, just as he had been.

Of course those days were over, but his age, which was erecting an opaque barrier between himself and Martha, was not so advanced that he did not want, nor appreciate, her sympathy.

'Not because I was hurt,' he said, picking up her question. 'Because we lost.'

Martha looked concerned, perhaps a little too much so. 'Well,' she said, 'you've lost before.'

'Yes.' Jan nursed his cheek. 'But this was the semi-final of the Cup, *The Cup*, and we were winning. It wasn't even my fault that we lost. It was the dust. I would have taken the ball *easily* but for that.'

'Ah, dust,' Martha said in a tone of voice which suggested that there was nothing about dust she needed telling. She ran her finger along the window ledge and held out her hand, her fingertip ochre. 'And I cleaned the whole place this morning,' she said. 'It's the mines,' she added reproachfully.

But then, curiously, Jan went on the offensive. 'We need those mines,' he said. 'If it wasn't for that gold, South Africa wouldn't exist.' He leaned back feeling a little better for having ticked off Martha. It wasn't for a black, even one as nice as Martha, to criticize the gold-mines.

Suitably chastened, Martha agreed. 'That's right, Master Jan. But you lost the match because of it, didn't you? Because of the dust.'

'Maybe,' Jan said sullenly, and went to his room.

Supper wasn't a joyous meal, and Jan was glad when it was over and he could leave the oppressive silence of the room, but when he was at the door his father shouted after him.

'No television for you. Go and play with some dolls.'

Jan wandered disconsolately on to the veranda. Already the street lights were on, blinding arc-lamps shining on the thorn hedges and the bungalows like lights along a prison wall. There was no one on the road. When darkness took possession of the city, people stayed indoors behind their thorn hedges, guarded by their ferocious dogs and their burglar alarms and their guns. And if they did go out, to a party or a film, they went in their cars, making darting forays into the night like scouts from a beleaguered fortress.

At Jan's heel, Bok growled as a police car went past. Half-way down the road it stopped and beamed a spot-lamp on a shadow; then it drove slowly off and the road was deserted again, lifeless except for the dogs barking at the conquering darkness.

Jan went to his room. The numbness was wearing away from his face which was beginning to throb. He peered into the looking-glass. A bruise was developing, a purple stain like a badge of dishonour. He lay on his bed, listlessly finger-ing a book, replaying the fatal pass over and over again, and thinking, apprehensively, of the coming Monday.

Outside Bok barked, car doors slammed, the front door was opened, there were voices and the chinking of bottles: guests arriving. Jan recognized their voices – predictable visitors ('The Gang' Mr Vorster called them), the women housewives and the men foremen in the mines, as was Mr Vorster himself.

On Saturdays they took it in turns to hold parties and, although Jan did not know what they did elsewhere, he knew exactly what they would do tonight: the women would sit in a corner and swap recipes and complain about servants, and the men would sit around the table, drink, play cards, and argue about sport and politics – although argue was hardly the word to use about politics since they were absolutely agreed on that topic. South Africa was right and the rest of the world was wrong; the blacks (Kaffirs they called them) were either children, savages or idiots, or all three combined, and never, ever, ever, would they be allowed equality with the whites – although this night Mr Vorster had a reservation about that.

'If the rest of the kids are like that son of mine,' he

boomed, his voice carrying through the bungalow, 'if they are anything like him, then this country won't last twenty years. Do you know what he did today?'

His voice ground on and Jan sighed. He supposed he would hear the tale of the dropped pass for the rest of his life. He tried to close his ears, but the tale was told and retold at intervals until the party broke up.

Boozy voices called good-nights. Martha cleared the sitting-room. Mr Vorster put Bok on his long running-chain in the back garden. Martha finished her work, and the back door was locked and bolted behind her as she went to the shed at the end of the garden which was her home.

Jan washed his face gingerly, brushed his teeth, muttered a good-night to his parents and went to bed. He drifted into an uneasy sleep from which he awoke after an hour or so, wincing as his bruised cheek rubbed on the pillow.

He got up and, without bothering to put on his light, dabbed cold water on his face. For a moment he stood looking through the window – and saw a shadow slip across the garden.

Jan blinked and the shadow had gone, but shadows in the night were not to be ignored. He peered into the moonlit garden. The night was still. The wind had died away and no bushes waved dark signals.

What, then, had he seen? Jan wondered. An animal? But the shadow had been too tall to be a dog or cat, and the only other animals in Johannesburg were human. And that was a thought to bring terror to a white South African, each and every one of whom was haunted by the fear that (although in fact it was an occurrence as rare as Halley's Comet) one night it would be their turn to awaken in the night and to see, looming over them, a black man with a knife.

For a moment Jan was tempted to wake his father. But

137

first he cautiously opened the window, and in the garden Bok growled.

Jan shook his head. He was seeing things. If there had been anyone, or anything, in the garden, Bok would have had it by the throat. 'All right, Bok,' he said, closed the window, and went back to bed.

Mrs Vorster was a devout believer in the sanctity of the Sabbath, which meant no games or television, so Sundays usually seemed interminable, but for Jan the next day passed like lightning, each rapid minute bringing closer his return to school and the undoubted scorn and disgrace.

And so it seemed the day had ended before it had begun, and Jan stood again in his room, peering into the night. But there were no sinister, flickering shadows in the garden, though Jan would almost have welcomed an attack by black hordes or, failing that, an earthquake.

No hordes attacked, no earthquake shook down the Paul Kruger School, and the next day Jan found himself walking through its gates and facing the undiluted ill-will of his fellow students. Assembly was worse. When, quite unnecessarily it seemed to Jan, the Principal read out the result of the match, a strange hissing echoed through the Hall and the teachers made no attempt to stop it.

But the awful thing, the truly awful thing, was that Jan quite understood the feeling of the school and, in fact, shared it. If the school, and Afrikanerdom, had two religions it was by no means certain that rugby came second, and it really did seem to him quite proper to be cast as the Judas who had, by that fatal fumble, betrayed the school – dust or no dust.

Just as Sunday had passed like lightning, Monday ticked away like a prison sentence. Shunned by his fellows, glared at by his masters, given a blistering tongue-lashing by the coach, Jan returned home a gloomy and dejected boy and spent a gloomy and dejected evening.

The next day his face was worse. In fact, the swelling was so bad that Martha insisted that he was too sick to go to school.

'Not like that, Missis,' she said to Mrs Vorster. 'Look at him, he should see a doctor.'

Mrs Vorster sighed and agreed. 'If it's no better this afternoon I'll take him,' she said. Jan did not know whether to feel glad or sorry. Not to go to school meant at least a day free from obloquy, but it also could be, and almost certainly would be, interpreted as moral cowardice.

At ten, Mrs Vorster went off to a coffee morning with friends. Slightly bored with himself, Jan sat in the kitchen with Martha.

'A day off that school,' Martha grinned. 'Not so bad, hey? It's a long time since you were sick. Not since you had the measles.'

Jan agreed. It had been years and years ago but, then too, as he had got better he had spent long hours in the kitchen with Martha, listening to the tales of the lizards and spiders, picking up a few Zulu words and phrases and, yes, enjoying himself. Martha was always cheerful – though that was understandable for, as Mrs Vorster often said, 'Why shouldn't she be happy? She's got a good job and a good master and, anyway, blacks are like that, not able to see beyond the next minute.'

At eleven Martha made coffee, gave Jan cake and called in Bok for his daily meal. Bok came in, docile but with his permanent air of restrained savagery.

'He's a good dog, isn't he?' Jan said.

'Bok? Oh ja,' Martha said a little doubtfully.

'Ja,' Jan echoed Martha, but with more conviction. 'If

any thieves came around here he'd have them, wouldn't he?'

'Have them?' Martha nodded. 'He'd have them by the throat. I tell you, I wouldn't want to be a burglar round here.'

'Right,' Jan said. And then, 'Have you ever seen a burglar, Martha?'

'Me?' Martha took a step backwards. 'Seen a burglar, those bad men? Of course I haven't, and I don't want to, either. Why do you ask such a thing?'

'Well,' Jan leaned forward, 'I thought that I saw someone in the garden the other night.'

'Saw –?' A look of genuine fear crossed Martha's face, leaving it ashen.

'Oh, it's all right.' Jan felt strong and protective. 'There's no need to be frightened. If there was a burglar Bok would have him – you just said so yourself. And then father would hear, and he's got a gun.'

'Yes,' Martha said. She gave a nervous giggle. 'You just gave me a fright, that's all. Seeing bad men in the garden at night.'

'I only said that I *thought* I saw something,' Jan said. 'I didn't say I did see anything.'

'No, that's right,' Martha said. She hesitated, her fingers trembling a little. 'Have you told Baas?'

'No,' Jan said. 'Should I?'

Martha fumbled with a dishcloth. 'I don't know. If you did see a bad man then you should. But if it was only a shadow ... well ... you know Baas.'

Jan agreed with that. He knew his father all right, and he wasn't the sort of man who would take kindly to being bothered with tales of shadows seen, or perhaps imagined, nights previously.

'Maybe I won't,' he said.

'Ja, I think that's best.' Some of the colour had returned to Martha's face. 'He'll think that you're seeing ghosts!'

Seeing ghosts ... Jan smiled, a superior smile. That was why Martha was so alarmed, she would be afraid of ghosts and spirits! All blacks were – he was sure of that, although she was the only black he knew.

'Yes.' Martha suddenly bustled around the kitchen. 'Now, Master Jan, I've got to go to the store.'

Jan found himself bundled out of the kitchen, and the back door banged as Martha hurried out. Left to himself, he wandered around the bungalow for a while, poking aimlessly into drawers and cupboards; then, finding nothing that he had never seen before, went into the back garden with Bok at his heels. It wasn't much of a garden – a scruffy lawn, a tiny swimming-pool, a barbecue – nothing much because the Vorsters weren't rich, Mr Voster being merely a working man. So Jan was bored there, too.

But Bok was restless. He snuffled about, whining, and Jan was mildly intrigued. He had seen Bok behave like that when the family had gone for picnics on the veld and he had scented another animal.

'Go on, Bok,' Jan said. 'Go on boy. Fetch it.'

Excited by Jan's voice, Bok growled and rooted among the fatigued bushes which leaned against the high fence that defended the Vorster home from the park, and then padded across the garden to Martha's hut.

Jan was a little exasperated. 'Come away,' he ordered. 'Come away, Bok!'

Bok looked over his shoulder but stayed where he was, one huge paw clawing at the door.

'Ach!' Jan took hold of Bok's spiked collar. 'What's the matter with you? That's Martha's hut.'

Bok pricked his ears at the sound of Martha's name but stood his ground, snuffling at the base of the door, a glint of fang showing. And then Jan felt a prickle of apprehension.

Slowly, very slowly, he stepped backwards, and further backwards, until he was within a safe distance of the bungalow – standing on the back doorstep, in fact – and then he took a careful look at the shed.

The shed, Martha's home, a blistered and faded green, built in exact conformity with the law (more than twenty feet from the road and with a window more than six feet high, so that white eyes would not be offended by the sight of a black servant resting), was as familiar to Jan as his own room. But now, in the bright sunlight, with its high blank window and with Bok growling ominously at the door, it seemed sinister, as if it might contain a secret, and not a pleasant one. It occurred to Jan that he was alone.

For a moment he was tempted to dash inside the bungalow and bolt the door behind him, but then he felt foolish. What possible danger could there be in Martha's old shed? Martha herself had spent the night there, and certainly no villain, no *tsotsi*, no black criminal, had crept in during the morning. And yet why was Bok scratching so frantically at the door?

And then Jan did what he thought was a brave thing. He got a stepladder, placed it against the side of the shed and climbed up.

He knew that he was doing wrong. The hut was the only scrap of privacy Martha possessed and Mr Vorster had always insisted that she be allowed it. For all his often brutal manners, Mr Vorster's belief in apartheid – the total separation of the races – was sincere, and he held to it with a certain crude justice. On the many occasions when Mrs Vorster had wanted to pry into the shed, he had flatly forbidden her.

'No,' he had said. 'That place is Martha's. Separate devel-

142

opment. It means what it says. She in her place and we in ours. Not for us to go poking around as long as she does nothing wrong.'

And so, since no one in the Vorster home ever dreamed that their Martha could ever do anything wrong, that was that: although Martha knew every nook and cranny of the Vorster home, no Vorster had ever been in Martha's shed.

But, with Bok snuffling and growling and baring his fangs, Jan – feeling virtuous and brave and with the heart-breaking ignorance of youth – climbed the stepladder and peered through the window. And ten seconds later he was back in the bungalow with all doors locked and bolted and frantically dialling a number on the telephone.

Black with grime from the gold-mine and still in his overalls, Mr Vorster was at the bungalow within thirty minutes, but not before the police cars, two of them and a van, had arrived with a wailing of sirens and screeching of brakes. When he charged from his car he found the garden full of white police-men with pistols drawn, an Alsatian with a black dog-handler who was looking nervously at Bok and, inside the bungalow, his hand protectively on Jan's shoulder, an officer who iden-tified himself as a Lieutenant Hendrick.

'What the hell's going on here?' Mr Vorster shouted, his face white beneath the grime.

'Mr Vorster?' Hendrick held out a calming hand. 'No need to be alarmed, everything is in order.'

'Order?' Mr Vorster's eyes bulged. 'There's a bliddy army out there!'

'Not an army.' The Lieutenant peered through the win-dow at the policemen crouching nervously among the bushes. 'Your boy here rang us. We have reason to believe that there is an intruder in that shed.'

'An intruder?' Mr Vorster stared incredulously at Jan. 'You rang the police?'

Hendrick cut in before Jan could answer. 'Yes, and a good thing he did. This could be a serious matter, very serious.' He managed to sound calm and excited at the same time.

'And ... but ... Well, why haven't you been in there?'

Hendrick sniffed disapprovingly. 'The key to the shed. You've got one, haven't you?'

'Yes. Yes, of course.' Mr Vorster fumbled in a bureau. 'Here it is.'

'Good.' Hendrick took the key. 'You see, we don't want to do any damage. Not if we can avoid it. We're here to enforce the law, not to break it.'

He cautiously opened the window. 'Mangula,' he said, 'Constable Mangula.'

The black constable darted from behind the barbecue and there was a whispered conversation through the window. Mr Vorster turned to Jan.

'If this is some idiotic stupidity,' he said, 'I'll break your neck.'

Further threats were left unsaid as Hendrick hissed at them to be quiet. Mr Vorster clamped his lips together grimly as Hendrick carried on speaking to the dog-handler.

'You understand, Constable? You take this key, go to that shed, open the door and put the dog in.'

There was a pause, then an unenthusiastic voice said that it did understand.

'Right,' Hendrick said. 'Keep low and make a dash for it.'

There was another pause and then a hoarse whisper. 'Baas.'

'Yes?' Hendrick said.

'That man in there. He might have a gun.'

'Don't you worry about that,' Hendrick said. 'The other officers will cover you. Now get on with it.'

He turned with a resigned shrug. 'Now you two had better get into the front room, just in case there is any shooting.'

He ushered Mr Vorster and Jan out, but in the hall Mr Vorster stopped. 'Did you say that there might be shooting?' he asked.

'There might be,' Hendrick said. 'You never know.'

'But Martha – the maid –'

'She's not in there,' Hendrick said. 'Now go and lie down. It will all be over in five minutes.

Obediently, Mr Vorster and Jan went into the front room and lay down behind the sofa. And so Jan missed the interesting sight of Constable Mangula covered by a battery of pistols, nervously approaching the shed, fumbling with the key but opening the door, diving to one side as he shoved his dog in, then shrugging, following him to reappear a moment later shaking his head and saying that there was no intruder.

'No intruder!' Mr Vorster bared his teeth and made a dive for Jan, but Hendrick blocked him off with the ease of long practice.

'Just you calm down,' he said in a voice which meant it. 'No, there isn't an intruder but,' he nodded meaningfully, 'but we've found something very interesting. Very interesting indeed, and you'd better come and see it.'

He led the way into the garden and into Martha's shed. Mr Vorster stared around. It was merely a shabby room: a narrow cot, a table and chair, an open Bible, a photograph nailed on the wall of two intensely respectable old black people, a small wardrobe, and –

'Oh,' said Mr Vorster. 'Oh, I see.'

'Yes,' Hendrick said with deep satisfaction. 'Clever of your lad to spot it, hey?'

And yes, Mr Vorster agreed with that. It was clever of his

fine, upright, brave, intelligent son to spot it. The other policemen agreed that it was clever, too (the white policemen that is – the black constable had been bundled back into his van). Mrs Vorster agreed too, as did the neighbours who had gathered outside the bungalow.

In fact, everyone agreed except Martha, who had been picked up at the bus stop for Soweto Township and who now stood in the kitchen, her face wet with tears.

'I smoke it,' she sobbed, as Lieutenant Hendrick waved under her nose the corn-cob Zulu pipe which Jan had so cleverly spotted through the window of the hut.

'Smoke it.' Hendrick nodded. 'Without tobacco. Smart trick that. And this,' he pointed to a man's hat which *he* had cleverly spotted in the wardrobe, 'do you wear this in the house when you are smoking your pipe without tobacco? And the fingerprints – do you have two sets of fingerprints which are all over your shed?' This, as Jan knew, was a lie because no fingerprints had been taken, but which, Jan supposed, was the sort of clever, necessary lie the police had to use to trap criminals, and which, if it was, proved a successful trap because Martha broke down and cried in anguish.

'He is my man! My man.'

'Your man?' Mr Vorster was aghast. 'You had a man . . . in my shed?'

'Aah, Baas,' Martha gave a long, moaning sob. 'I'm sorry.'

'Sorry!' Mr Vorster stepped back as though Martha had some contagious disease and stared at her with loathing. 'You brought a man into my shed?'

'Yes.' Martha raised her fine head. 'But he's my husband, Baas. My lawful wedded husband. We're married, in church. It's no crime, Baas.'

But it was. It was a crime. And cheerful, willing Martha

146

was arrested, hustled out to a police car and driven off to police headquarters.

'I can't believe it,' Mr Vorster said, shaking his head over a glass of brandy. 'I've been so good to that woman.'

'They are like that,' Hendrick said over his brandy. 'No gratitude. You can't trust any of them. Believe me.'

'Right.' Mr Vorster brooded for a moment. 'But how did they get away with it? I mean, in a city like this, police every-where – no offence, Lieutenant.'

'None taken.' Hendrick indicated that another glass of brandy would be acceptable. 'We can't be everywhere. It's a bit like stopping the tide you know, build a wall here and it breaks through there. But you can see how he got here. Out of Soweto, through the dumps, chancing his arm across the park . . . it can be done.'

'But Bok!' Mr Vorster said. 'He's out there all night, and I'll tell you, if a lion came into that garden he'd have it – no?'

'No,' Hendrick shook his head. 'Think about it. Who knows your dog best? Who was with it every day and all day, and fed it? Right – your maid. So when her man came, she just went out and soothed it. I keep two dogs myself,' he added conversationally, 'a Doberman outside and a fox terrier inside. Good barkers those terriers. Well . . .'

He strolled out on to the veranda. 'We'll see that park gets a better patrol,' he said. 'Oh, and by the way, sorry we had to bring a black along, but you know how it is. Well, see you in court. A good lad you've got there. A hero really.'

And, somewhat to his amazement, that was what Jan seemed to have turned into. From being a virtual pariah he was a hero! His picture was in the paper, with a story saying how a brave Afrikaner boy had discovered and foiled some sinister and immoral plot. At school he was an even bigger hero. In fact, the Principal praised him at Assembly and Jan never forgot his words.

'A model for you all,' the Principal told the students. 'Brave, resourceful and intelligent. Our country, South Africa, need fear nothing while we have such youths as our guardians.'

And Martha? She was found guilty of harbouring a black man in a white area, thus breaking innumerable laws, and ordered to be transported to a remote homeland she had never seen before. And there she lives now, slowly dying in a harsh and arid country.

And her husband? That man without a reference book, the pass which might have allowed him to live and work in the country in which he had been born? The police did not find him, and so, no doubt, he lives his illicit, fugitive life somewhere among the millions of blacks who toil and labour in his beautiful land.

But he and Martha are of no real importance, you know. What is their little tale among so many others? They are mere specks, mere specks of dust in a desert, that is all.

But, when you think of it, specks of dust can do terrible harm, can't they?

Beginners

MICHELLE MAGORIAN

THE scene was over. The stage was plunged into black-out. Tony turned swiftly and headed for the nearest opening in the wings, aiming for a strip of white tape which had been stuck on the wooden floor.

One of the actors ran past him and flung back the door leading to the corridor. For a brief moment, a shaft of light exposed Tony's mother who was standing, waiting for him.

Tony stopped at the tape and stared down at it, ashamed. He was so appalled by what he had done on stage that he was certain he would never be allowed into a theatre again. He glanced sideways at the prompt corner. Sue, the deputy stage manager, was perched on the high stool, leaning over the prompt book and giving a lighting cue into a small microphone. He didn't know whether to thank, apologize or curse her.

He took a step, hesitated, and then stumbled back towards his mother.

She swung back the door to the corridor and put her arm round his shoulders, but he couldn't bring himself to look at her. A deep ache welled up into his throat causing his nose and eyes to sting fiercely.

One of the actors strode past them, a shabby duffel coat over his faded corduroys. He was playing the Social Worker in the next scene.

'You handled that prompt well,' he remarked. Tony whipped his head round but he had already disappeared into the wings.

He had forgotten that the play was relayed backstage over the Tannoy system. That meant the rest of the cast must have heard him being prompted from their dressing rooms.

His mother gave him a squeeze. 'Come on, love,' she murmured. 'Let's get back to the dressing-room.'

He walked beside her, his hands shoved in his pockets. And still he wouldn't look at her. He couldn't. And anyway, she wouldn't understand. Not like Brian's mother.

They turned up the curved stone steps which led to his dressing-room – the dressing-room he shared with Annie. He couldn't be in one of the men's dressing-rooms because his mother had to remain with him. She was employed as the theatre chaperone for both him and Brian. They had to have one. It was the law. And it was the law that he was only allowed to do so many performances a week, which was why the theatre had to have two boys playing the same part on alternate nights.

His mother pushed open a door off the first landing. Tony paused for a moment in the doorway and took in the two

150

mirrors on the far wall surrounded with lighted bulbs and 'good luck' cards, the table with make-up and tissues spread out on it, the small chipped sink in the corner, the old threadbare armchair, the tatty rug on the floor, the rail with his and Annie's change of clothes hanging from it.

Annie had explained how the lights around the mirrors gave an idea of how one's make-up would look under stage lighting. Tony didn't need much make-up, just some base and a bit of mascara because his lashes were so fair, but half way through the play he had to look as though he hadn't had much sleep. Arthur, who had been fifty years in the theatre, had shown him how to make up a mixture of greasepaint in the palm of his hand so that he could thumb-in shadows under his eyes.

As he gazed at the greasepaint sticks Arthur had lent him, he remembered what he had done. How could he face Arthur now?

He walked towards his dressing-table pulling off his sweater, and sank into the chair.

'You'd better get changed,' said his mother.

He raised his head and looked at her in the mirror. She was holding out a school uniform.

'Yeah,' he said dismally.

He took it from her and slung the blazer over the back of the chair.

Feeling a mixture of numbness and pain, he slipped on the grey shirt and knotted the stripey tie. He kicked off his sneakers, unzipped his jeans and stepped into the long grey flannels. Before he could swallow the tears back, they rushed down his face. He brushed them aside angrily and sat down to put on his lace-ups.

His mother drew up her chair beside him. 'Don't take it to heart, love. There's other nights.'

'I've only got four performances to go.'

He tugged hard at the laces, blinking away the blur in his eyes.

'I don't understand what happened. It was only when I saw everyone staring at me that I realized it was my turn to speak. And then I went completely blank. Even after I'd been prompted I forgot how to do it. It felt like I was improvising. It was a shambles.'

'It sounded fine. Funnily enough, it sounded better.'

'How could it?' he muttered. He shook his head. 'Now they'll never ask me to work here again. It'd be all right if there weren't two of us playing the same part. It's not fair. Brian gets all this extra help.'

His mother gave a sigh. They had been through this discussion before. Many times. She picked up a bundle of knitting from the corner of the table and sat back.

'Why won't you help me?' he asked.

'I've told you. I'm not a director.'

'Neither is Brian's mum and she coaches him before every single performance.'

'I test your lines, don't I?'

'Yes, but you don't tell me how to say them.'

'That's the director's job.'

'But he never tells me either. He just talks about what kind of boy Andrew is, and his feelings, and that I just need to listen to the others and then reply. When I try and put in a gesture like Brian, he tells me not to do it. That's what mucked everything up tonight.'

His mother lowered her knitting.

'What do you mean?'

'I did this arm movement Brian's just put in. It completely threw me.'

'You were trying to copy Brian?'

'Yes.'

'But why?'

'He and his mother know more about the theatre than I do, so he must be doing it better.'

'Don't be daft. You were picked at the audition, same as him.'

He swung round.

'Mum, be honest. Do you think I got the part just because I'm small?'

'There were plenty other small ones there.'

'But most of them were eleven, like the character.'

'There were other thirteen-year-olds, too,' she pointed out. 'You got picked because you were good enough. Now tie your other shoe-lace up.'

He bent over and tightened it. He wished he could believe her, but she didn't know anything about acting and the theatre. All she seemed to care about was the money angle. He remembered with embarrassment how she had written off to some place in London as soon as he'd been offered the part, and the next thing he knew, she'd asked the Management to pay him and Brian more money. He nearly died, especially when Brian's mother said she didn't want anything to do with it, and that Brian would be only too glad to have the honour of performing in this new play for nothing. He had gone through agonies while the Management were making their decision, terrified he would lose the part.

There was a knock at the door.

He straightened up quickly.

It was Graham and Arthur. Tony reddened.

'Thought we'd pop in to see you,' said Graham. 'Heard you looked a bit down.'

'Yeah,' whispered Tony, glancing down at his hands.

'It's not because you dried, is it, old fellow?' boomed Arthur.

He nodded.

'Join the club,' said Graham. 'We've all done that.'

Tony looked up.

'Oh, yes,' added Arthur, 'me too.'

They came into the dressing-room. Arthur sat in the armchair and leaned forward intently, his hands clasped.

'I'm afraid we weren't much help,' he commented.

'Usually someone can feed you a line,' said Graham, 'but everything you were saying was supposed to be a revelation. And we all had to be dumbstruck.'

'Arthur, have you really dried too?'

'Worse. When I started out in weekly rep I was once playing two characters in the same play, and was so tired one night that I did my quick change too soon. I was just about to rush on when I realized I was the wrong person. It was too late to change back so I had to stand in the wings and listen to my fellow actors having to make up the rest of the scene without me.'

At that moment Sue's voice came over the Tannoy. 'Mr Henderson and Mr Forsyth, this is your call, your call please, Mr Henderson and Mr Forsyth. Thank you.'

They leapt to their feet and made for the door. Just as Arthur was about to close it, he turned.

'By the way, old boy, I rather like the way you did the scene after that dry. More real.'

Tony stared after him, open-mouthed.

His mother smiled.

'There you are,' she said casually. 'They don't think badly of you.'

Tony listened to the Tannoy. The scene between the character Annie was playing and one of the people in the communal house was coming to an end.

He slipped on the school blazer. Annie would have walked off the set by now. She'd be hurrying into the wings and making for the corridor.

He sat on the edge of his chair and stared at the door in the mirror. As soon as he heard her running up the stairs he began to sweat.

His mother, observing him, said nothing.

Suddenly the door burst open and Annie rushed in, pulling off her jersey at the same time.

Tony looked away.

He was still smarting from the telling-off she had given him the previous week, when he had tried to tell her a joke just as she was about to go on stage. But he hadn't meant to upset her. On the contrary, he wanted to impress her. 'Never, never do that again,' she had raged. 'The time in the wings is preparation time. You're working with a professional company now. I expect you to behave like a professional.'

Now he took a deep breath.

'Sorry about the prompt,' he blurted out.

'You handled it like a pro,' she remarked.

Tony whirled round.

She had changed into the baggy green trousers and voluminous red sweater ready for their last scene together. He watched her tuck her long auburn hair into a short wig.

'Aren't you angry?'

She separated a grip with her teeth and slid it in behind one ear.

'No. It's an awful thing to happen to anyone.'

'But everyone in the audience must have heard it.'

She sat back and looked at him. 'But you didn't fall apart at the seams. You picked it up and carried on as though nothing had happened.'

'I had to. It's an important scene.'

'Yes. You cared more about saving the scene than nursing your own bruised ego.'

'What's an ego?'

She laughed. 'You'll find out soon enough if you stay in this business.'

'You mean you think I might be good enough to be a professional actor one day?'

She touched his arm. 'Is that what you want?'

He blushed. 'More than anything else in the world.'

'Oh dear. You have got it badly.'

'You make it sound like a disease.'

'It is.'

She let go of his arm and applied some fresh lipstick to her mouth.

'Do you think,' he began hesitantly, 'I'm as good as Brian?'

She looked quizzically at him.

'He really worries you, doesn't he?'

'Yes.'

'Just because he gives a different performance it doesn't make his better or worse. You're different people. You couldn't possibly play it the same way.'

'But he's so good technically. I mean his mother is always helping and . . .' He stopped.

The two women glanced at one another.

Annie turned back to the mirror, smacked her lips together and tissued off a smudge.

'Yes. Brian has quite a problem there,' she muttered.

Tony stared at her.

'A problem? But she helps him.'

'She hinders him, Tony.'

'But he was word-perfect on the first day of rehearsal. Not like me.'

'Or me,' she reminded him. 'Or Arthur, or anyone else. We learnt our lines as we rehearsed the play. Acting is about working with other people, not doing a solo spot with them.'

'But he says his lines so clearly and makes fantastic gestures.'

She turned to face him.

'Tony, I know technique is important. I mean, if a deaf old lady has paid for a ticket at the back of the theatre she wants to be able to hear what's going on. But if there's no heart . . .' She paused. 'I'm not saying Brian has no heart, but when he's on stage with me I feel his mother's with us too. I can see him desperately trying to remember her latest instruction. His eyes glaze over as though he's reading a manual inside his head. Sometimes it's so bad I can't even make eye contact with him. It's terrifying for him. She really winds him up. I'm only thankful she's not allowed backstage during the performance.'

'I thought it was a rule that no one was allowed.'

'It is. But his mother was hoping to be the chaperone on his performance nights. We soon put a stop to that.'

Tony was flabbergasted.

'What do you mean?'

'We all got together and begged the director not to allow it. Luckily for us, your mother agreed to be one for both of you.'

'Mum! You never said.'

'And a bloody good chaperone she is too,' continued Annie. 'He's a bag of nerves when he arrives. At least the poor little bugger has thirty-five minutes' peace before curtain up. It takes all that time for your mother to calm him down.'

Tony turned to his mother.

'Why didn't you tell me?'

157

'I was afraid it might get back to Brian. It'd upset him if he knew people weren't too fond of her. You won't say anything, will you?'

He shook his head.

'I thought you were doing the extra chaperoning for the money. I thought you were doing everything for the money.' He paused. 'Like all that stuff about my wages.'

'Have you heard yet?' asked Annie.

Tony's mother nodded.

'Perhaps tonight would be a good time to tell him.'

'What's going on?' said Tony, eyeing them suspiciously.

His mother drew out a piece of paper from her handbag. It was a typed form.

Below the words British Actors' Equity Association was written APPLICATION FOR CHILDREN'S TEMPORARY MEMBERSHIP. His mother had filled in his name and address and the repertory theatre and production underneath.

'I didn't want to say anything till it had arrived. I had to send off a copy of the contract to London first. That's why I asked them to raise your pay. If you earn half of what the adults get, you can apply for child membership. It's only temporary, but if you do any other acting jobs in the next few years then, when you're sixteen, you can try and get something called your provisional card. It's ever so hard to get that one and you can't get work without it, so . . .'

'You mean I'm sort of a Junior member of the Actors' Union?'

'If you want to be. If you sign this form. It's up to you.'

'Oh Mum,' he breathed.

'I'm not pushing you to be an actor, don't think that. But if later on that's still what you want, then there's no harm in helping things along a bit.'

Tony sat back and grinned.

'Got a Biro?'

Annie picked one up from her dressing-table and handed it to him.

'Sure you know what you're doing?' she asked wryly.

He nodded happily.

Below where he was supposed to sign was another dotted line for the signature of a parent or guardian. Tony scribbled his name above it and slid the form towards his mother.

'Your turn now, Mum.'

'There,' she said, after signing it. 'I'll put it in the post tomorrow.'

Annie stood up and took an old raincoat from the rail.

'By the way,' she said, 'I know you dried in that scene, but afterwards, it was the best you'd ever played it. What happened?'

'That's what Arthur said!'

He caught sight of his mother suppressing a smile. 'And Mum.'

Just then Sue's voice came softly over the Tannoy. 'Ms Masterson and Mr Wilson, this is your call, your call please, Ms Masterson and Mr Wilson. Thank you.'

'Let's go,' said Annie.

As the three of them walked down the steps together, Tony turned over Annie's question in his mind. What *had* happened to him in that scene which had made it so different? Then it clicked. Usually he was always criticizing himself from outside, conscious of what he was doing with his arms and his voice. After he had been prompted he had thrown himself totally into the scene. And he had *believed* in what was happening! That was the difference.

They stepped through the door into the wings. He and Annie walked to the back, out of sight of the prompt corner.

On the floor beside a makeshift gate was a wooden cue-board with two small red and green light bulbs on it.

In the shadows Tony gazed at Annie. Already she had started to look different. And then she wasn't Annie any more. She was Gwen Simpson, the single woman in her thirties who had moved out of the communal house where she had been living, because some of the House members had vetoed a child living in their communal set-up.

And he was Andrew, the eleven-year-old boy who was only meant to have stayed with her for a fortnight while his parents went away for a holiday – a holiday from which they never returned.

He could feel the tension leaving his body, and in its place, exhilaration.

The lights dimmed. The stage crew changed the set to a sparsely furnished sitting-room. The red 'warn' light came on for Annie. She raised the collar of her raincoat and picked up the bags of shopping which had been set there for her.

One of the assistant stage managers, a young man, stood by the gate. The green light flashed. He opened and slammed the gate, and Annie stepped on to a makeshift gravel path which led to the porch.

The red light was on for Tony's entrance. There was a sound of heavy rain. The assistant stage manager pumped water through a punctured hose which had been attached above a window, so that on stage it looked as though the rain was trickling down the glass.

Tony picked up his duffel bag, and the assistant stage manager sprayed his face with water.

The green light flashed on.

Tony slammed the gate and ran like fury up the path.

Black-out. He and Annie dashed into the wings. Behind

them the lights came up again for a curtain call. Covered in custard and mashed potato and soaked from a water fight, they laughed at one another.

'That's the best we've ever done it!' panted Annie.

'It was fantastic!' he cried.

'*You* were fantastic. What happened?'

'I suddenly realized what the director was going on about. That they'd had to keep everything bottled up for months and they didn't have to do it any more because they had a place of their own. They didn't have to hold it all in till the next house meeting. They could just go mad.'

'You enjoyed smashing all that china tonight, didn't you?'

'Yeah.'

'Me too.'

She glanced on stage.

'Come on, it's our turn now.'

The rest of the cast had been taking their bows. He and Annie walked downstage centre and the applause grew louder. Everyone joined hands and the cast took a bow together. Arthur was holding Tony's other hand. As they lowered their heads Tony heard him whisper, 'Well done, old boy.'

As soon as the curtain came down, everyone except Annie and Tony fled off stage for the dressing-rooms. He and Annie strolled into the wings, their arms around each other, still glowing from the last scene. Tony's mother was holding the door open for them and beaming.

Out in the corridor Graham and Arthur dashed past them, their coats under their arms.

'Half a lager?' shouted Graham to Annie. 'Or a pint?'

'A pint please. I could drink a river.'

'G'night Tony. See you on Tuesday. G'night Jane,' he added, waving to Tony's mother. 'Have a good weekend.'

161

Annie ran up the stairs, Tony and his mother following on slowly.

Tony glanced aside at her, at the soft fine lines round her eyes that deepened when she smiled. Annie was right. She was a good chaperone. She didn't crowd him. Even when he got ratty with nerves, she just let it wash over her as if she understood.

'Mum, were you nervous about taking the chaperone job?'

'Terrified. I'd never met professional actors before, let alone worked in a proper theatre.'

'Like me eh?'

'Yes.'

He slipped his arm round her waist.

'Was I really good tonight? See, I couldn't tell.'

'Not bad.' She smiled.

They stopped outside the dressing-room door.

'How about me, then?' she said. 'Was I a good chaperone?'

He grinned and strolled nonchalantly into the dressing-room.

'Not bad.'

Secrets

ANITA DESAI

ONE morning, at school, Rohan got every single sum wrong. Then he dropped a bottle of ink on the floor and it splashed on to his teacher's white canvas shoes. When he made a face behind his teacher's back, he was seen. So he had to be punished.

'Here, take this letter to your father and go home,' his teacher said, after writing a long and angry letter. 'Let him punish you as well.'

Rohan tried to look too proud to care, and picked up his books and walked out of the school yard and up the narrow city lane. But once he reached the big grey banyan tree that was the only tree in the lane, and found that the cobbler who usually sat under it, mending broken old shoes, was not there, he sat down in its shade, hiding himself in the folds of the great trunk, and sobbed a little with anger. He had not been able to get his sums right although he had tried. He had dropped the ink bottle by accident and not to spoil the teacher's white shoes. Perhaps it was bad of him to pull a face but how could he help it when things were going so badly? Now he was afraid to go home and hand the letter to his father, who would be very angry and beat him. He sometimes did, and often scolded him.

So Rohan hid there in the folds of the grey tree-trunk, and poked with a stick at the seeds dropped on the ground by the parrots that ate the red berries of the tree. He was so angry and afraid that he poked and poked with the stick till he had dug quite a deep hole in the dust. In that hole he found a little grey lump of rubber – a plain piece of rubber that some other schoolboy might have dropped there long ago. He picked it up and rolled it about between his fingers.

'I wish it were a magic rubber,' he said, sobbing a little. 'I would rub out the whole school, like this – like this –' and he stepped out to look down the lane at the boys' school that stood at the end of it, and angrily rubbed at the air with the grey lump of rubber.

Then he stopped, his hand still in mid-air, his mouth still open, and his hair began to stand up on his head as it did on his neighbour's cat's back when she saw his dog.

Something very, very strange had happened. The school had vanished. He had really rubbed it out! The tall, three-storeyed house on its left, with its latticed balconies and green roof, was still there, and on the other side the tin-roofed warehouse where timber was stacked stood there too, but in between them, where the school had been, there was now a patch of earth. There was no white school building, no deep verandas, no dusty playground, no high grey wall and not a single schoolboy. There was just a square of bare brown earth between the other buildings, all quiet and still now in the heat of the afternoon.

Rohan's knees were shaking. He ran a little way down the road to see better but still could find nothing but a blank where the school had once been. Then he felt so afraid of the vanished school that he ran back up the lane as fast as he could, snatched up his books and the terrible rubber from among the roots of the banyan, and ran into the road where he lived. He hurried up the stairs at the side of the little yellow house to their room on the roof where his mother hung the clothes to dry and his father stacked old boxes and bicycle tyres.

His mother was alone at home. She was kneading dough in a big brass pan. The fire was not yet lit. 'You're early,' she said, in surprise. 'I haven't any food ready for you yet. But you can go and break up an old box and get me some wood to light the fire. I'll warm some milk for you. Hurry up, don't look so sulky,' she said, and began to roll and thump the dough in the pan, roll and thump, roll and thump, so she did not see the face Rohan made as he went out to pull an old crate to pieces and bring in an armload of packing-case wood.

He came in and threw it all into the grate with such force that the ashes and grit flew up and settled on all the pots and pans, and the dough and the neat floor as well.

His mother was so angry, she shouted, 'What's the matter with you, you rascal? Look what you've done! What a mess you've made! Now go and fetch the broom and sweep it up at once.'

'I won't sweep,' he shouted back, as loudly as though there were a devil in him, shouting for him.

She was still more angry. 'I won't sweep it up either. Let it lie there and then your father will see it when he comes home,' she said.

Then Rohan felt so afraid that he held up the magic rubber and cried, 'I won't let you do that. I won't let him see it. I'll – I'll rub you all out,' and he swept through the air with that little grey lump of rubber, as hard as he could. He shut his eyes tight because his face was all screwed up with anger, and when he opened them the whole house with the unlit fire, the brass pan, the glass of milk and even his mother had vanished. There was only the roof-top, blazing in the afternoon sun, littered with empty tins and old tyres at the edges but quite, quite bare in the middle.

Now Rohan did not have a home or a mother or even a glass of milk. His mouth hung open, he was so frightened by what he had done. Then he turned and ran down the stairs as fast as he could, so that his father would not come and find him standing alone on the empty roof-top.

He heard an excited bark and saw it was his dog Kalo, who had been sleeping in the shade of an overturned basket in a corner of the roof-top, but had heard him run down the stairs and followed him. Kalo was frightened, too, at the way their room had disappeared and the roof-top left standing empty, so he was running along behind Rohan, barking with fright.

Rohan felt afraid that the people who lived in the yellow house would come out and see what had happened, so he shouted 'Go back Kalo! Go back!' But Kalo ran towards him, his long black ears flapping as he ran. So Rohan rubbed the air with his rubber again and screamed, 'I don't want you! Go away!' and Kalo vanished. His round paw marks were still to be seen in the dust of the road. A little trail of dust was still hanging in the hot, still air of that dreadful afternoon, but Kalo the dog had vanished.

And someone had seen. An old man who traded in empty tins and bottles had just started his evening round and, while shouting 'Tin and bo –' stopped short and stared till Rohan, rubbing in the air with his rubber again, shouted, 'You can't see! You mustn't see!' and rubbed him out. That old man with his grey beard and big sack of clanking tins and bottles just disappeared as Kalo had.

Then Rohan turned and ran even faster. He ran into the big road that went round the mosque. Just in time he remembered that he might meet his father there, for he had a cycle repair shop at the foot of the mosque steps. So he whirled around again. He kept going in circles, as if he were a little mad. At last he ran to the banyan tree, climbed over its roots into a cleft between two folds of the huge trunk and hid there, trembling.

'I'll hide this terrible rubber,' he said at last. 'I'll put it back in the hole and never, never take it out again.' With shaking fingers he scraped more dust from the little hole he had dug earlier, in order to bury the rubber.

As he scraped and dug with trembling fingers, he found something else in the hole. At first he saw only one end of it – it was long and yellow. He dug harder and found it was a pencil. Quite a new pencil – he could see no one had used it before, though it looked old from being buried in the earth. He stopped crying and trembling as he wondered who could have buried a pencil here, and whether it was a magic pencil as the rubber was a magic one. He had to try it and see.

First he dropped the rubber into the hole and covered it up. Then he held up the pencil and pointed it at the bare patch of earth where the school had once stood between the warehouse and the green-roofed house. Very, very carefully he drew a picture of his old white school building in the air. He did it so carefully that he seemed to see the grey lines forming before his eyes. Then he blinked: the grey-white building really *was* there now. Or was it only a picture in his mind? Quickly he drew the verandas, the playground, the high wall, and then the little matchstick figures of a line of schoolboys rushing out of the front gate, the lane filling with them, and saw them leaping and running with their satchels flying behind them.

He stood up and ran a little way down the lane, out of the shade of the mysteriously whispering banyan tree. Now, in the clear sunlight, he could see the school quite plainly again, alive and noisy with children set free from their lessons. He stood there till he saw the teacher come out on his bicycle. Then he turned and ran the other way up the lane.

He stood in the middle of the dusty road and quickly, quickly, drew a picture of a little black dog in the air, as well as he could. He was still working on the long plumed tail when he heard Kalo bark, and saw him bounce down on to the road on his four feet and come pelting towards him.

As he came closer, Rohan saw he had missed out the jagged edge of Kalo's ear where it had been torn in a dog-fight. He was careful to add that so Kalo would be exactly as he had been before, scarred and dusty and wild with happiness. Kalo stood still, waiting for him to finish.

When it was done, he shouted 'Kalo! Kalo!' and patted him hastily, then went on busily with his pencil, drawing the old, bearded tin-and-bottle man. He was just drawing the big, bulging sack when he heard the cracked voice cry '-o-ttle man!' and there he was, shuffling down the road and blinking a little in the bright light.

Then Rohan and his dog ran home, up the stairs to the empty roof-top. There, leaning against the low wall, his tongue between his teeth and his eyes narrowed, Rohan drew a picture of his home as well as he could. Even when he could see it quite plainly, the little whitewashed room with its arched windows and pigeon-roost on the flat roof, he went on drawing. He drew a picture of his mother kneading dough in a pan, the fire, the glass of milk and even the broom in the corner of the room. Then he went in and found them all there, just as he had drawn them. But he saw one mistake he had made in his drawing – he had coloured his mother's hair black and left out the grey strands over her ears. She had remained stiff, lifeless. He stood in the doorway, rubbing gently at the unnatural darkness of her hair till it showed the grey he knew. He realized you cannot draw a picture out of desperation, or with careless speed. It took care, attention, time.

When he had finished, his mother moved, looked up at him. 'There's your milk,' she said quietly, 'drink it up.'

He nodded. 'I'll sweep up a bit first,' he said, and went to fetch the broom. He swept and he swept, enjoying the work that he had not wanted to do at first, till he heard his father arrive, lean his bicycle against the wall and lock it, then come slowly up the stairs.

Rohan ran out, shouting 'Look, I found a pencil and a rubber on the road today.' He wanted so much to tell his father all about it and ask him how it happened, but he did not dare.

His father was looking tired. 'Why don't you sit quietly and draw something?' he said, as he went in for his tea.

Rohan nodded and went to fetch a piece of paper. Then he sat on the top step and spread out the paper and drew. He was not sure if the magic pencil would draw an ordinary picture. It did. Using it very, very carefully now, he drew a picture of Kalo.

When his father saw it, he beamed. He had never seen a picture as good. Rohan showed it to his mother too, and she was so pleased she pinned it on the wall, next to the calendar.

His father said, 'I didn't know you could draw so well.

169

Your teacher never told us. You should draw a picture for him.'

Rohan spent the whole evening drawing with the magic pencil. He took the drawings to school next day, and his teacher was so pleased with them that he forgot to ask for an answer to his angry letter of the day before. He gave Rohan good paper and time to draw every day.

Rohan drew so much that the magic pencil was soon worn to a stub. Instead of throwing it away like an ordinary pencil, he took it down to the banyan tree and buried it in the earth at its roots where he had hidden the lump of rubber. As he walked away he worried about whether he would be able to draw as well with an ordinary pencil bought at the stationery shop near the school gate. But he had had so much practice now, and become so good an artist, that he found he could do as good a drawing with the new pencil he bought as with the magic one.

He became so famous in that town that people came from miles away to see the pictures his mother pinned to the walls of their house. They went to the school and asked the teacher about him. No one knew how he had learnt to draw and paint so well without any lessons or help. Even when he became a great artist, whose name was known all over the land, Rohan did not tell anyone the story. That was his secret – and the banyan tree's, and they kept it to themselves as secrets should be kept.

The Guard Dog

DICK KING-SMITH

CHAPTER I

THERE were six puppies in the window of the pet shop. People who knew about dogs would have easily recognized their breeds. There was a Labrador, a springer spaniel, an Old English bobtail, a poodle and a pug.

But even the most expert dog-fancier couldn't have put a name to the sixth one. In fact most of those who stopped to look in the pet-shop window either didn't notice it (because it was so extremely small), or thought it was a rough-haired guinea-pig (which it resembled in size and shape) that had got into the wrong pen.

'What on earth is that?' the rest had said to one another when the sixth puppy was first put in with them. 'Looks like something the cat dragged in!' And they sniggered amongst themselves.

'I say!' said the Old English bobtail puppy loudly. 'What are you?'

The newcomer wagged a tail the length of a pencil-stub. 'I'm a dog,' it said in an extremely small voice.

The pug snorted.

'You could have fooled me,' said the poodle.

'Do you mean,' said the Labrador, 'you're a dog, as opposed to a bitch?'

'Well, yes.'

'But what sort of dog?' asked the springer spaniel.

'How d'you mean, what sort?'

The pug snorted again, and then they all started barking questions.

'What breed are you?'

'What variety of dog?'

'Why are you so small?'

'Why are you so hairy?'

'Are you registered with the Kennel Club?'

'How many Champions have you in your pedigree?'

'Pedigree?' said the sixth puppy. 'What's a pedigree?'

There was a stunned silence, broken at last by a positive volley of snorts.

'Pshaw!' said the pug. 'He's a mongrel!'

At that they all turned their backs and began to talk among themselves.

'I say!' said the Labrador. 'D'you know what I'm going to be when I grow up?'

'A gun dog, I bet,' said the springer spaniel, 'like me. I'm going to be a gun dog and go out with my master and bring back the pheasants he shoots.'

'No,' said the Labrador, 'as a matter of fact I'm not. I'm

going to be a guide dog for the blind. A much more worth-while job.'

'No more worthwhile than mine,' said the Old English bobtail. 'I'm going to work sheep. I'll be galloping about all over the countryside ...'

'... getting filthy dirty,' interrupted the poodle, 'while I'm having my coat shampooed and specially trimmed and clipped, and a silk ribbon tied in my topknot. I'm going to be a show dog and win masses of prizes.'

The pug snorted.

'What about you?' barked the others. 'You haven't said what you're going to be when you grow up.'

'I am going to be a lap-dog,' said the pug loftily. 'I shall be thoroughly spoiled and eat nothing but chicken and steak, and the only exercise I shall take will be to walk to my food-dish. Pshaw!'

'What about me?' said that extremely small voice. 'You haven't asked me what I'm going to be when I grow up.'

The Labrador yawned. 'Oh, all right,' it said. 'Tell us if you must.'

'I,' said the sixth puppy proudly, 'am going to be a guard dog.'

At this the others began to roll helplessly about, yapping and yelping and snorting with glee.

'A guard dog!' they cried.

'Mind your ankles, burglars!'

'He's not tall enough to reach their ankles!'

'If he did, those little teeth would only tickle them!'

'Perhaps his bark is worse than his bite!'

'It is!' said the sixth puppy. 'Listen!'

Then out of his hairy little mouth came the most awful noise you can possibly imagine. It was a loud noise, a very,

very loud noise for such a tiny animal, but its volume was nothing like as awful as the tone of it.

Think of these sounds: chalk scraping on a blackboard, a wet finger squeaking on a window-pane, a hacksaw cutting through metal, rusty door-hinges creaking, an angry baby screaming, and throw in the horrible bubbly sound of someone with a really nasty cough. Mix them all up together and there you have the noise that the sixth puppy made.

It was a dreadful noise, a revolting disgusting jarring vulgar noise, and it set all the creatures in the pet shop fluttering and scuttering about in panic. As for the other puppies, they bunched together as far away as they could get, their hackles raised, their lips wrinkled in loathing.

At last, after what seemed an age, the sixth puppy stopped. Head on one side, he wagged his pencil-stub tail.

'You see,' he said happily in his usual extremely small voice. 'I can make quite a rumpus when I really try.'

CHAPTER 2

'Nobody will buy him,' said the other puppies later. 'That's for sure.'

'What a racket!' said the sheep-dog.

'It made me feel quite ill!' said the gun dog.

'A really common noise!' said the guide dog.

'Made by a really common animal!' said the show dog.

'Pshaw!' said the lap-dog.

They all stared balefully at the guard dog.

'The sooner he's sold, the better,' they said.

And that afternoon, he was.

Into the pet shop walked a tall lady with a face that looked as though it had a bad smell under its nose, and a small fat girl.

'I am looking for a puppy,' said the lady to the shopkeeper, 'for my daughter. I know nothing about dogs. Which of these would you recommend?'

All the puppies lolloped forward to the inner wire of the pen, whining and wagging and generally looking as irresistible as puppies do.

All, that is, except the guard dog. He sat alone, small and silent. He was not exactly sulking – that was not in his nature – but he still felt very hurt.

'Nobody will buy him. That's for sure,' they had said.

He resigned himself to life in a pet shop.

The shopkeeper was busy explaining the various virtues of the five pedigree puppies when the fat child, who was standing sucking her thumb, took it out with a plop. She pointed at the guard dog.

'Want that one,' she said.

'Oh, that's just a mongrel puppy, dear,' said the shopkeeper. 'I expect Mummy would prefer . . .'

'Want that one.'

'But darling . . .'

The small fat girl stamped her small fat foot. She frowned horribly. She hunched her shoulders. With a movement that was as sudden as it was decisive, she jammed her thumb back in her small fat mouth.

'She wants that one,' said her mother.

By the end of that day, the guard dog was feeling pretty pleased with life. To be sure, there were things about his new owners that he did not quite understand. It seemed, for example, that simple pleasures like chewing carpets and the bottom edges of curtains drove the lady into what he considered a quite unreasonable rage, and as for the child, she was temperamental, he thought, to say the least.

175

Though at first she had seemed willing to play with him, she soon began to complain that his teeth were too sharp or his claws too scratchy or his tongue too slobbery, and had made a ridiculous fuss over a doll which had sported a fine head of hair and was now bald.

Strange creatures, he thought that night when at last all was quiet, but I mustn't grumble. I'm warm and well-fed and this seems a very fine house for a guard dog to guard. Which reminds me – it's time I was off on my rounds. Ears cocked, nose a-quiver, he pattered off on a tour of the down-stairs rooms.

His patrol over, he settled down in a basket in the kitchen. There was plain evidence that he had done his duty. In the centre of the drawing-room, for example, there was a fine white fleecy rug, and in the centre of the rug was a bright yellow pool. In other rooms there were other offerings.

Comfortable now, the guard dog closed his extremely small eyes. It had been a tiring day, and he was just drifting off to sleep when suddenly, outside the kitchen door, he heard a stealthy sound!

He leaped to his feet.

CHAPTER 3

Afterwards they could not understand why their cat would never again enter the house, but lived, timidly, in the garden shed. They did not know that its nerves had been shattered by the simple act of pressing against the cat-flap, something it had done every day of its life. This had resulted instantly in a noise that sounded to its horrified ears like a number of cats being scrunched up in a giant mincer. Upstairs, the fat child woke screaming, and soon her mother came rushing down those stairs and stepped in something unusual at the bottom.

Even then the guard dog might still have had a house to guard (for it was difficult for them to believe that so little a creature was capable of making so ghastly a noise), if only he had kept his mouth shut next morning. But he stuck to his task, challenging everything that seemed to him a threat to the territory which it was his duty to protect.

Quite early, at the sound of whistling and the chink of bottles outside the door, he woke his owners once more. And no sooner had they taken the milk in than the postman knocked, and they actually saw the guard dog in action.

Happily unaware of the effect of his voice upon the human ear, and mindful only of his role – to give warning of the approach of strangers – the guard dog kept it up all morning. The cleaning woman (who found a great deal of cleaning to do), a door-to-door salesman, the electricity man come to read the meter and a Jehovah's Witness were each in turn greeted by the dreadful medley of sounds that emerged, full blast, from the guard dog's tiny throat. Last came a collector for the RSPCA, the rattle of whose tin inspired the guard dog to his loudest, longest and most furious outburst.

'RSPCA?' screamed his distracted owner. 'What about a society for the prevention of cruelty to people?' And by midday, as she unscrewed the aspirin bottle, she said to her daughter, 'I'm sorry, darling, but I cannot stand that row a moment longer. It'll have to go. Will you be very upset?'

The small fat girl, her eyes fixed malevolently upon the guard dog, did not even bother to remove her thumb from her mouth. She merely shook her head, violently.

That afternoon the guard dog found himself, to his surprise, in a very different kind of home, the Dogs' Home. He could not make out what had gone wrong. What were guard dogs meant to do if not guard? He had only done his duty, but all he had so far received had been angry looks and angry words before finally they bundled him into their car, and drove him to a strange place full of strange dogs and left him.

From the kennel he had been given, Number 25, he looked around him. There was every sort of dog in the kennel block, young and old, handsome and ugly, large and small (though none remotely as small as he). Why were they all there?

'Why are we all here?' he asked the dog directly opposite him, a sad-looking animal with long droopy ears and a long droopy face.

'Because,' said the dog dolefully, 'we are all failures.'

I don't get it, thought the guard dog. My job is to give warning of the approach of strangers. I've never yet failed in that.

'I don't think I'm a failure,' he said.

'Well, you're certainly not a success,' said the long-faced dog, 'or you wouldn't be here. All of us are here because our owners couldn't stand us any longer.'

'But we'll get new owners, won't we?'

'Possibly. It depends.'

'Depends on what?'

'On whether you take someone's fancy. You just have to do whatever you're best at. Me, I'm best at looking sad. Some people like that.'

In the days that followed, many people in search of a suitable pet came to inspect the twenty or so current inmates of the Dogs' Home; and when they came to the end of the range of kennels and found the smallest inhabitant, they would without exception break into smiles at the sight of so charming a little scrap.

Without exception, however, they were treated to the dreadful spectacle of the guard dog doing what he was best at.

And without exception the smiles vanished, to be replaced by looks of horror, as they turned away with their hands clapped to their ears.

By the time the guard dog had been in the Dogs' Home for a week, most of the animals had gone happily (or in the case of the long-faced dog, sadly) away with new owners, and there were newcomers in most of the kennels. By the thirteenth day, there was only one dog left of those who had been there when he was admitted. This was his next-door neighbour, an old and rather smelly terrier.

The guard dog's attempts to make conversation with it had always thus far been met with a surly growl, so that he was quite surprised when he was suddenly addressed.

'You bin in 'ere thirteen days, littlun, an't you?' said the terrier.

'Oh,' said the guard dog, 'have I?'

'Ar. You come in day after I. 'Tis my fourteenth day.'

'Oh well,' said the guard dog, 'try not to worry. I'm sure you'll soon be gone.'

'Ar,' said the terrier. 'I shall. Today.'

'But how can you know that? How can you know that someone's going to take you away today?'

'Fourteen days is the limit, littlun. They don't keep you no longer than that.'

'Why, what do they do with you then?'

'An't nobody told you?'

'No.'

'Ar well,' said the old terrier. ''Tis all right for us old uns, 'tis time to go. I shan't be sorry. You don't feel nothing, they do say. But 'tis a shame for a nipper like you.'

'I don't undersand,' said the guard dog. 'What are you trying to tell me?' But though he kept on asking, the old dog only growled at him, and then lay silent, staring blankly out of its kennel. Later, a man in a white coat came and led it gently away.

CHAPTER 4

'Oh thanks,' said the manager of the Dogs' Home, when one of his kennelmaids brought in his cup of coffee at eleven o'clock next morning. He looked up from his record book.

'Shame about that little titchy one in Number 25,' he said.

'You don't mean . . .?' said the kennelmaid.

''Fraid so. If things had been slack we could have kept him longer, but the way dogs are pouring in, we must keep to the two-week rule. He's one for the vet today.'

'Oh dear,' said the kennelmaid. 'He's such a lovely little fellow. Dozens of people fell for him, until . . .'

'. . . until he opened his mouth,' said the manager. 'I know. It's a pity, but you can't blame them. In all my long experience of every sort of dog, I've never come across one with such a dreadful voice. Nobody could possibly live with that – though talk about burglar alarms, any burglar would run a mile if he heard that hullabaloo. And you wouldn't need to dial 999, they'd hear it at the nearest police station, easy.'

The guard dog ate a hearty breakfast, and was a little surprised, when the kennelmaid came to clean out his run, at the fuss she made of him. She cuddled and stroked and kissed him as if she would never see him again.

Then he remembered what the smelly old terrier had said. This is my fourteenth day, he thought. Great! Someone will pick me out today!

He sat, waiting for the time when the public were admitted, determined that today of all days he would leave no one in any doubt as to the quality of his greatest asset. Other guard dogs, he supposed, might act in other ways, by looking large and fierce (which he could not), or by leaping up and planting their feet on the shoulders of burglars and suchlike and knocking them flat (which he most certainly could not). He had only his voice, and when the door to the kennel block opened he let rip, *fortississimo*.

No one even got to smiling at him that morning. Everybody kept as far away as possible from the dreadful sounds issuing from Number 25, and concentrated upon the other inmates. The guard dog was left strictly alone.

When at last the batch of would-be owners had left, some with new companions, some empty-handed, all mightily relieved to reach the comparative peace and quiet of the busy roaring street outside, the guard dog sat silent once more. There was a puzzled look on his extremely small hairy face.

Can't understand it, he thought, nobody seems to want a decent guard dog. But if fourteen days was the limit, then they'd jolly well have to find him somewhere to go today. Perhaps the man in the white coat would take him too – he seemed a nice sort of chap.

He watched the door to the kennel block.

It was not the man in the white coat who came in but the kennelmaid, and a white-haired man who walked with a stick with a rubber tip.

'Would you like me to come round with you?' the kennelmaid said, but he did not answer, so she went away and left him alone.

The old man walked slowly along the row of kennels, looking into each carefully with sharp blue eyes. At last he came to Number 25.

Outside the door, the kennelmaid stood listening, her fingers tightly crossed. But then she heard that fearful noise start up and shook her head sadly. She went back into the kennel block to find the old man squatting on his heels. There was a grin on his face as he looked, apparently totally unmoved, at the howling bawling yowling squalling guard dog. He levered himself to his feet.

'I'll have this little fellow,' he said firmly. 'He's the boy for me.'

'Oh good!' cried the kennelmaid. 'He's lovely, don't you think?' But the old man did not answer. He did not reply either, later, when he had paid for the guard dog and the kennelmaid said, 'Would you like a box to carry him in?' And in answer to the manager's question, 'What are you going to call him?' he only said, 'Good afternoon.'

Light suddenly dawned on the manager of the Dogs' Home. He stood directly in front of the guard dog's new owner so as to be sure of catching his eye, and said deliberately, in a normal tone, 'That's some dog you've got there. The worst voice in the world!'

The old man put his hand up to his ear. 'Sorry?' he said. 'Didn't catch that. I'm as deaf as a post and I can't be bothered with those hearing-aid things, never been able to get on with them. What did you say?'

'That's some dog you've got there. The best choice in the world!' said the manager very loudly.

The white-haired old man only smiled, leaning on his stick with one hand and cradling his purchase in the other.

The manager shouted as loud as he could, 'He's a dear little chappie!'

'See that he's really happy?' said the old man. 'Of course I will, you needn't worry about that. We'll be as happy as two peas in a pod.' He fondled the puppy's extremely small hairy ears. 'Funny,' he said, 'I fell for him though he wasn't actually what I was looking for. I live all on my own, you see, so really it would have been more sensible to get a guard dog.'

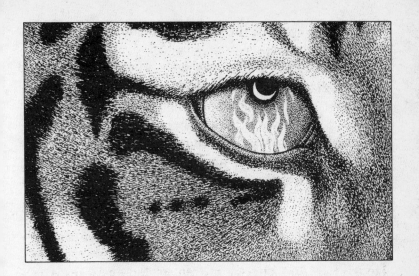

The Guardian

TED HUGHES

MAN was easy to create. God simply shaped the clay, breathed life into it, and up jumped Man, ready to go.

God smiled. 'Now,' he said, 'I'll make your better half. Then you'll be complete.'

So then God shaped Woman. He took great care, and she turned out perfect. God was pleased. But when he tried to breathe life into her – nothing happened. He tried again, breathing the life in very gently. She just lay there, lifeless clay. He shook her slightly, and frowned.

Man was watching anxiously. 'What's wrong?' he cried. God didn't answer. He only rolled Woman up into a ball between his palms, and started all over again.

This time he took even more care. And pretty soon, there she lay, more perfect than ever. So once again, God kneeled forward, and breathed life into her, more warmly and gently even than before.

Still nothing happened.

There she lay, warm from God's hands, perfectly shaped. Much more perfect than Man. But lifeless.

Man couldn't hold back any longer. 'Let me have a go!' he cried, and almost pushed God aside. He grabbed Woman by the shoulders and began to shake her. 'Wakey wakey!' he called. 'Come on! Time to go!'

Her limp body shook like a rag doll, but her eyes stayed shut.

All at once he seemed to grow angry. His hair began to fly, he ground his teeth, his eyes blazed, and God was suddenly afraid what might happen as Woman's arms flapped and flopped, and her head joggled and rolled. He caught Man's arm and jerked him away. 'Steady on!' God shouted. 'She's fragile!'

But Man began to pound the earth with his fists. 'I can't bear it!' he cried. 'Do something. She's my other half. You can't just leave her lying there on the cold ground.'

God stared at him hard. Easy enough to say 'Do something,' but if life wouldn't go into this marvellous new creation of his, then it wouldn't go, and that was it. He didn't know what else he could do.

At that moment, a small bird flew down and landed on Woman's left big toe. 'Let me have a try,' said the bird. 'I have magic.'

It was the Nightingale. Nightingale had a most peculiar voice. God looked at this slim, brown, tiny creature and remembered all the trouble he'd had with the voice-box. Nightingale's voice-box was incredibly complicated. God had been struggling to get this voice-box right. And then,

184

one night, it had come to him in a dream. The perfect voice-box! And it solved one of his toughest problems: how to get the voice of the seven seas into an organ the size of a common house-fly. And there it was in his dream. He'd woken up with a jolt, and snatched it out of the air before it could vanish. He got it – but grabbing it like that, half asleep, he'd broken it.

And what a job that had been, trying to start it up again inside the bird's tiny throat. Still, it just about worked, finally. But the voice, wonderful as it sounded, was obviously only the bits and pieces of something much more tremendous.

'Try if you like,' sighed God, and he watched gloomily as Nightingale perched on Woman's nose and began to sing.

Man had never heard the Nightingale sing. And now it really let itself go, he couldn't believe his ears. As it sang, his eyes grew very large and round. Suddenly they closed, his head dropped forward on his chest, and he was in a trance.

And a row of eight Monkeys, sitting on the branch of a tree above him, fell to the ground, bounced once, and lay still, eyes closed, in a trance.

What singing!

But Woman never stirred. And though Nightingale flung out his chest, and fluttered his wings, and though his throat was a blur of throbbing song, Woman simply went on lying there, like a heap of clay.

'No good!' cried God. He clapped his hands and Nightingale flew startled into a bush.

As God clapped his hands, something else moved. A snake, the deadly Puff-Adder, lifted his head. He had actually been lying tucked in under Woman's side for the warmth of God's hands that was still in the clay. And now he peered over her waist, his forked tongue dancing, and said:

'I think I can solve your problem. I think I can awaken this perfect person.' And his long mouth seemed to smile.

God eyed the Puff-Adder anxiously. He didn't trust this snake at all, with its eye-chips of granite. He was almost sorry he'd made it. When he'd pressed those eyes into place one had cut his thumb, and the wound had festered for days.

'Under Woman's heart,' said Puff-Adder, 'lives a Frog. It got in there with the clay you used. You didn't notice.'

God was surprised to hear that.

'I can smell it,' said Puff-Adder, 'through her ribs.' And he flickered his dancing thread of a tongue over Woman's chest. 'Here it is.' He tapped with his nose to show the exact spot.

'This Frog,' he went on, 'simply sucks up all the life you breathe into her. As you breathe the life in, the Frog swells up. Look.'

And it did seem to God, as he looked more closely, that Woman's stomach was slightly swollen there, under her heart.

The Puff-Adder laughed. 'Now,' he said, 'watch me extract it.'

And he began to glide up beside Woman's throat, and over her chin and was just about to slide his blunt strange head between her parted lips when God caught his tail and threw him into a stiff little thorn-bush nearby.

The Puff-Adder yelped with pain. 'You'll pay for this!' he cried. 'I would have picked that Frog out in no time. Then you could have breathed life into Woman and she would have lived. But now – now – now –'

'Well?' roared God. 'Now what?'

The snake was silent.

'I know you,' God shouted angrily. 'You'd have got in there, and eaten the Frog, if there is a Frog, and then just curled up in its place. That's what you'd have done. And you'd never have come out again. You'd have been a thousand times worse than any Frog.'

The Puff-Adder gave a wild laugh. Then it hissed: 'You're right. I would. But at least Woman would have come to life. And what a life! She and I together – we'd have conquered the world! We'd have driven you out among the furthest stars. Man would have crawled after us in the dust.'

God was furious. He didn't know what to think. Had the snake told the truth? Was there truly a Frog under Woman's heart? A Frog that sucked up the breath of life as he breathed it into her?

He stared at Man, lying there in a trance among the Monkeys. And he stared at the faint bulge under Woman's beautiful, lifeless ribs, and he gnawed the soft inside of his lower lip.

God advertised for help. 'Divine Rewards for whoever can make Woman live.' The creatures talked about little else. Every day, somebody came with an idea. None worked. And Woman went on lying there, perfect and lifeless.

Till one day, as God sat in his workshop, with his head in his hands, pondering this great problem, he heard a rustling voice.

A familiar voice!

He lifted his head. Whose voice was it? And what was it saying? Surely he knew that voice! Then a strange expression came over his face and his heart began to thump. He twisted round, and now he heard the voice clearly. It was coming from under a dusty heap of workshop rubbish, in that far corner.

'I can help you,' it whispered. 'I have the answer.'

In two strides he was across the room and lifting the rubbish aside, carefully, piece by piece. The dust rose and the gloom was thick. But at last he saw. He put one hand flat on the ground, and bent even lower, and peered. Yes, there she was – embedded in rubbish, like a crab under a flat rock – his own little Mother!

He'd completely forgotten her!

Gently he lifted her, and carried her out into the middle of the room. She was a great knot of doubled up arms and legs, like a big, dry, dusty spider. And almost weightless! He set her down, ran out and came back with a glass of brandy. She smacked her wet, blackened lips, and her eyes glittered. She smiled up at him, easing her joints slowly.

'I know your problem,' she said. She half closed her eyes, and seemed to rest a little. Then she said: 'First, bring me the New Moon.'

That was easy for God. He reached down the New Moon.

He watched as she half crawled over the floor, lifted the cellar hatch, and disappeared down the dark hole, with the New Moon cupped in her hand. He peered after her. He'd never dared lower himself into that place. But it had always been his Mother's favourite den, in the old days. And now suddenly her skinny hand rose up out of it again, holding the New Moon like a bowl – a bowl that was brimful of dark liquid.

'Take this,' said her voice out of the darkness. 'Put it in your kiln. Just as it is. And stoke it very hot. The hotter the better.'

As God took the New Moon in his hand, a little waft of fear touched him. Usually the Moon was icy cold, but now it was warm. What was in it? Was it what he thought it was? He bent closely to sniff. Was it blood?

How was this going to help him?

But his Mother had always known best, in spite of her oddity. So God did as he was told. Taking care not to spill it, he put the New Moon into his kiln. He sealed the door, and began to stoke the fire beneath. The flames roared up.

As he went on sliding logs into the blaze, God began to feel very happy. It was just like old times, when his Mother was teaching him how to do things. 'The hotter the brighter the brighter the better,' he sang to himself. He almost forgot about the cold clay shape of Woman away there in the forest, and Man stretched out in a trance, under a tree, among the Monkeys. And all the time the kiln glowed brighter. Soon it seemed to be throbbing, and almost transparent, the colour of apricot, with pulsing spots of dazzling whiteness. 'Can I get it white hot?' he whispered. 'Hotter hotter brighter brighter better better –' But at that very moment the air seemed to explode in his face:

WHOOOOF–

The whole kiln had exploded and God fell over backwards with his eyebrows blown off.

And as he fell, something flashed above him, out of the explosion, like a long flame streaked with black.

He sat for a while, looking at the reeking crater where the kiln had been. Then as he got up, knocking the fiery, smouldering splinters from his hair and beard and muttering, 'Well! I'm sure that wasn't supposed to happen! What a mess!' he suddenly felt uneasy and looked round.

A strange animal stood there, watching him. A lanky, long, orange-red beast, painted from one end to the other with black stripes. Its belly and throat were frosty white. Its pelt shone. It lashed its long tail and stared into God as if it saw something moving in there. It was like no creature he had ever seen.

But the strangest thing of all was what it held in its mouth.

'It's caught a Monkey!' was God's first thought. 'It's already started killing my Monkeys!'

But then he saw it wasn't a Monkey at all. It was a tiny Human Being! A baby Human Being!

Had this leapt out of the kiln? Was this his Mother's magic? How was this going to bring Woman to life? The tiny Human Being was quite nice, but that beast was more likely to frighten her to death. No, God could see his Mother's magic had got all mixed up. And now he remembered why he'd left her in the corner, and heaped the rubbish on top of her, and hired the beetles to feed her.

But the beast had turned its head. Holding the baby high, clear of the brambles and poison ivy, it went off through the forest, straight towards Woman. God began to run. He wanted to get to Woman first. But the beast began to bound. In three leaps it disappeared away ahead, in the thick jungle. Then God heard the cry of the Monkeys, and a strange, hoarse bark – not like Man at all, but God knew it was Man. And when he reached the clearing, everything had happened.

Man and the Monkeys were all together, on a high bough in the Monkeys' tree, staring down with eyes of fright. And the great beast stood over Woman's body.

As God watched, it laid the midget Human Being on Woman's stomach, stretched its own great striped length beside her, and began to lick her ear.

At once, the Baby began to stir its arms and legs. Its mouth opened like the door of a little kiln, and out of it came a thin cry.

The moment the Baby cried, the beast lifted its head and looked into Woman's face. And God, fascinated, looked at Woman's face. And the Monkeys in the tree, and Man beside them, all looked down at Woman's face. But the face remained quite still, quite lifeless.

After a while, the beast again began to lick Woman's ear gently, closing its eyes as it licked. And the wrinkled, podgy baby seemed to grow stronger, as if its cries were some kind of food. It shook its fists at the sky. It seemed to be shaking the bars of a cage.

All at once the beast leapt up and bounded away, so lightly it seemed to be weightless. And God saw it had the Baby back in its mouth. The beast stopped, sat down, and watched Woman. And the Baby hung in its mouth, silent.

God, too, watched Woman. Then he felt the hair prickle on the back of his legs. And a shiver crawled up his spine and into his hair. Woman's hand was moving. It came slowly to her head, till her fingers touched the bridge of her nose, where the Nightingale had perched with its sharp claws. She drew a deep breath and sighed.

Watching her very closely, the beast came back and laid the Baby on her thighs, and nudged it with its paw. At once the Baby opened its mouth and wailed. The air filled with its cry. And Man too, in the Monkeys' tree, let out a cry, 'Aaaagh!' and slid down the trunk to the ground. Then he scampered across to God, and peered out from behind him. And what he saw made him cry out again: 'Aaaagh!'

Woman was sitting upright, nursing the Baby. She bent over it, her hair hanging forward like a curtain. It had happened! And the beast lay at her feet, gazing at God and Man.

God was astounded. His Mother's magic had worked! But how? And what about that Frog? And what about the Baby? The Baby was a brilliant idea! Why had he never thought of it!

Wildly excited, God started forward, with Man clinging to the fringe of his apron. But the great beast rose to meet them. The hair on its shoulders lifted and spread like the tail of a peacock, its jaws opened, and a solid blast of sound hit them – a blast like the exploding of the kiln.

191

Man blew away like a straw, and God reeled stumbling after him, with his brain spinning. What was this beast? Was it a walking kiln exploding whenever it pleased? What was it?

'Do you know what you've done?' he cried, as he came gasping to his Mother. 'Do you know what you've let loose?' She was still squatting there on the floor, above the cellar hatch. She grinned, showing him all her gums, then put back her head and cackled. Her hands, dangling over her knees, and dancing and dithering there, reminded God of the black tongue of the Puff-Adder.

'That,' she crowed, 'is the Tiger. He's an Angel. He is the Protector of the Human Child.'

God was mystified. This was the first he'd ever heard of Angels.

'Look, Mother,' he said. 'Your Tiger or Angel as you call it – it's too much. He knocked me over with one shout. He shows no respect. He's too frightful. The Baby's all right. In fact, I don't mind the Baby at all. The Baby's good. But the Tiger's overdoing it. Please take him back.'

'Take him back?' she croaked. 'How?'

'Just take him back. If he scares me, what's he going to do to the rest of my Creation? He's too much.'

His Mother looked at God solemnly. 'The Human Child,' she said, 'needs an Angel Protector. And the Tiger's it.'

God flew into a tantrum. 'You need a Protector,' he yelled. 'Let him protect you. My world can't handle him. He doesn't fit. If the Human Child needs a Protector, let's have something I can cope with. Something that fits.'

His Mother flailed her hands loosely together – exactly, thought God, like an old chimpanzee. 'OK!' she laughed. 'OK. I'll have him back. It's done.'

Then she clapped her palms together over her head, and

192

held them there, fingers pointing upwards, elbows on her knees, while her face suddenly lowered and her eyes closed.

Fleeing from the Tiger's roar, Man had dived into a garbage pit. Hearing the laughter of God's Mother, he'd stayed there. But now he came creeping out, and saw God returning. They went together towards Woman.

She sat as they'd left her, suckling the Baby. Man ran to her, and squatting beside her reached out to touch her hair, and gazed at her with shining eyes. The Tiger had gone.

God stood stroking his beard. He looked first at Woman, then at the Baby, then at the small, gingery, striped animal that sat beside Woman's crossed ankles, gazing at Woman and the Baby with sleepy, half-closed eyes.

This creature looked quite like the Tiger, but it was only the size of the Baby. And after one sleepy glance, and one sleepy blink, it ignored God and Man.

'So what's this?' asked God, abruptly, pointing to the new creature.

Woman leaned her foot over, and the little animal rubbed its ear on her big toe. She wriggled her toes, and it pressed its chin on to them, laying back its ears and closing its eyes.

'This,' she said, 'is our Pusscat. We call him Tiger.'

God nodded thoughtfully. So this was how his Mother had solved the problem. But at that moment the Pusscat pricked its ears. An unfamiliar sound made God look up. It seemed to come from the clouds. No, it came from the mountains.

Steep-faced mountains surrounded the forest. A horizon of mountains. They looked like giant grey or brown or blackish faces, propped up in bed with the forests pulled up under their chins, like coverlets. Out of those mountains came a strange, echoing sound. A strange, clangorous cry, rising and falling. It was like a terrible singing. A dreadful sound really.

As he listened, God felt that same shiver creeping up from his heels into his hair. Just as when Woman's hand had moved. And he knew that this was the Tiger. He frowned. And his frown became almost a grimace. The voice of the Tiger seemed to take hold of his brain and twist it.

'Tiger!' he whispered. 'Yes, Tiger!'

As he said the word, he shivered again, and felt the hair actually stir on his head.

'Tiger!' he whispered. And the same weird electrical thrill came again. He gave a little laugh.

'Tiger!' he growled. Then again, more fiercely: 'Tiger!' His eyes opened wide. He felt his hair standing up on end. And before he knew it he was roaring out: 'Tiiiiigerrrrr! TIIIIIIgerrrrrrr! TIIIIIIIGERRRRRRRR!'

The echo of his roar came bounding and rumbling back off the mountains mingled with the appalling song of the animal. God stood there as the sounds rolled through him and over him. He had never felt anything like it. It was terrifying and yet, he had to admit it, it was wonderful. It was like nothing in his own Creation. It was wonderful in a whole new way. What was this strange new thing in his Creation?

The Tiger seemed not to have heard him. It flowed along, sometimes deep in the jungle gorges, sometimes high on the rough sides where forests hung over cliffs. Its body resounded like a giant harp, as the tree shadows and the sun's rays stroked over it. A tremendous, invisible song, it moved slowly around the mountain circle, full of its dark ideas.

God half turned and stared at the Pusscat. It occurred to him that the Pusscat too, whether it liked it or not, was breathing that sound. And Man too. And Woman, and the Baby.

Everything in his Creation was having to listen. Every creature in the thickets, every tiniest insect under the leaves, they were all breathing air that was trembling with the voice of the Tiger. Nothing could escape it. And his old Mother, she was breathing it too – probably still sitting where he'd left her, with her knobbly, shrivelled hands clasped over her head, and her head bowed, smiling into her closed eyelids.